To Mary,

Plum Pudding

with best wishes

from

Esther

Plum Pudding

a family guard book

compiled
by

Esther Herschel-Shorland

Published by Esther Herschel-Shorland
Crossingford Lodge, Doctor's Lane,
Pulham St Mary, Diss, Norfolk IP21 4RJ

Layout, design and typesetting by
John Halliday, The Old Maltsters,
Pulham St Mary, Diss, Norfolk IP21 4QT

Printed by The Ipswich Book Company Ltd
The Drift, Nacton Road, Ipswich, Suffolk IP3 9QR

ISBN 0 9531772 0 3

To my dear husband
John Herschel-Shorland
whose own family is well documented in guard books and
museums and who has made Crossingford Lodge into such
a lovely family home.

Esther Herschel-Shorland

Introduction

Life presents us with a rich mixture as in a plum pudding. As my 60th birthday approaches on 15th October 1997, I have tried to record some of the sweeter bits but occasionally a hard nut or bitter spice may intrude. This book is basically in order to celebrate my life at this point and to thank my family and friends for the helpful, entertaining and necessary roles they have played in it. Together we made the pudding, tasted it and found it good.

Thanks are due to John Halliday without whose advice, diligence and sensitivity the mixture would never have shaped up into a book.

Chronology

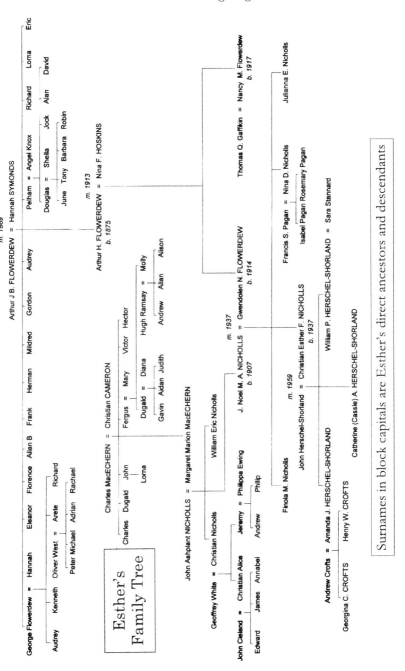

Esther's Family Tree

Surnames in block capitals are Esther's direct ancestors and descendants

'In Australia the swans were black ...'

In The Beginning

I was born a Cockney sparrow within the sound of Bow Bells but was taken out to Malaya at the age of six weeks. This was in 1937. My parents had been married in Kuala Lumpur on 15th January of that year and had chosen for their honeymoon, a trip home that took them around the world.

In Malaya I was looked after by a Chinese amah while my mother played the violin in an orchestra, and competed in tennis and golf tournaments by day, and my father, then Head of the CID in Singapore, raided opium dens and arrested murderers by night.

An early memory was of being chased around the garden by a mad monkey when I was two or three. The monkey had to be shot.

Tea parties were arranged for me and my little friends who each brought their amahs. My guests were served on Bunnikins china.

Daddy played the banjo and mandolin and sang cheerful songs. No wonder our fox terrier was called Dixie.

We went on leave to Australia flying on a seaplane. I felt very sick and was given barley sugars and cream crackers which helped. When we returned to Singapore I remember telling my amah proudly 'I'm three now!'

Gaff, who was my godfather, gave me a huge blackboard to draw on, I also had a set of Arthur Mee's *Children's Encyclopaedia*, and a big white teddy bear. All of these things and most of my parents' wedding presents were lost at the Fall of Singapore. That was when we had to hide in a dug-out that was made for us to shelter in when the Japanese bombers came overhead.

When that happened we never saw Dixie again, and my father was taken prisoner by the Japanese and interned in Changi. My mother, then pregnant, and I, then aged four and a half, were put on a ship to be evacuated to Australia. As he put me on board the ship my father gave me a beautiful sleeping doll, I also managed to take my bag of minibricks with me, and Cottontail the cuddly rabbit that my mother had made. I remember lifeboat drill on the crowded ship, and having to queue up with a bowl for a portion of food — my first experience of the British queue.

When we arrived in Australia we were taken to the Refugee Centre where I was issued with one toy, a grey felt elephant, and one book — about the adventures of Wonky an Australian koala bear. Then we went to live with my Flowerdew grandparents in Melbourne and soon Nina Dilys was born. Our Aunt Nancy helped to look after us. She sang to us, and took me ice skating which she was very good at. She also took me to my first performance of Gilbert and Sullivan, *The Gondoliers*, and to the *Desert Song*. She had a Scotty dog called Kiltie that her admirer Gaff had given her. I was photographed by the Melbourne newspaper racing along the beach with Kiltie on our earlier happier stay in Australia before the war.

My grandparents' pink house was by the sea. In the summer the sky was coloured pale ochre and terra cotta from the dust. My grandparents had a lovely garden with lemon trees and tiger lilies. Once I could not resist picking one of my grandfathers prize tiger lilies but he taught me a lesson with a sharp rap from his walking stick.

We used to go to tea with two elegant and refined elderly ladies called Ella and Chick Figgis who had a beautifully dressed Victorian china doll which they let me hold carefully and which prevented me from fidgeting as they talked to my mother.

I won first prize in the under eight years age group for a poster for the Victorian Society for the Protection of Animals. Kindness to animals had to be the theme, and the exhibition of work was opened by the Anglican Archbishop of Melbourne. This was in 1945.

In Australia the swans were black, and one snatched an ice-cream out of my hand! At school, arithmetic was taught with the aid of imitation chocolate frogs. One day while adding them up I popped one into my mouth. What a lesson that disgusting mouthful taught me — it wasn't real chocolate at all!

As a child in Australia I went to dancing classes where I wore the Cameron tartan kilt that my mother made for me, and learnt to dance the Highland Fling, and other Scottish dances to the tune of the Keel Row. I also learnt ballet steps to wartime popular tunes such as *Lily Marlene*, and *Don't Sit Under the Apple Tree with Anyone Else But Me* (... till I come marching home!)

When Nina Dilys was three and I was eight the war ended and we sailed to England to be reunited with my father. He and Dilys had never met before, but I was sure that I recognised him on the Liverpool quayside! We spent that night in my first hotel where everything in our room seemed to be a uniform green. It snowed as we travelled from Liverpool to London. Dilys and I had never seen snow before. What a contrast to the heat of Singapore's Changi Jail where the Japanese had kept my father a prisoner for the duration of the war. On his release the Red Cross had issued him with Harris tweed plus-fours, jacket, waistcoat and overcoat that were a warm Highland Bull colour and the scratchy feel and the smell of it tickled our noses.

To Cassie on reaching Singapore 1991

See J and E
Aged two or three
In Singapore
Before the war.

Here's J's new toy
For special boy –
And dog with E
The dear Dixie.

It was a time
Of golden clime,
When all was well
Before we fell.

We went to school
(It was the rule)
Beyond the sea.
Our family

Just sailed away
One sunny day
And we were left
Somewhat bereft

So photographs
Weren't just for laughs.
They showed us who
We mattered to.

The misty haze
Of early days
We can explore
Through photodraw.

The garland's scent
Is sometimes meant
To help remember
Spring in September

You have a new
Much later view.
The journey varies –
Life's bowl of cherries!

Celebrating the end of World War II

Thank you to Nancy who looked after me when I was little in Australia

When it was a time to rejoice
The flag was hung outside
The house in Melbourne.

When you brushed
Your long dark hair
You used to sing to me
Where e're you walk
And *Old King Cole.*

You used to help Granny
To look after me
When Mummy was ill
Or having the baby.

I did not like
Your Army uniform -
But you were a
Brave kind lady.

*Aunt Nancy and Esther
with the Union Jack*

75 Esplanade, Elwood
Melbourne, S.3
Australia

Esther's grandparents, Arthur and Nina Flowerdew, during the Second World War.
The recipe below is in Nina Flowerdew's handwriting.

Melbourne Pudding
1 cup flour – wholemeal or white
1 " breadcrumbs
1 " sugar
1 " finely chopped suet.
½ teasp baking powder
Mix all together – then add 1 tablesp. jam
Lastly 1 small teasp. baking soda in
small cup milk
Steam 2 hours – Serve with custard –

Esther and Dilys

Colours and clothes

During my childhood I was brought up at different times by each of my grandmothers. In Australia and Malaya I lived with the dainty little Nina Flowerdew who nearly always wore turquoise so I came to think of her as my 'turquoise grandmother.' She had a jaunty sea-green felt hat with a trembling feather that quivered and tickled my nose. My Nicholls grandmother, Margaret, wore a lot of pink and lilac so that I called her my 'purple grandmother'. She came in a larger size and was theatrical.

When we arrived in London just after the war there was clothes rationing so second hand clothes were sent to us from Hollywood by our highland grandmother, Margaret, who as yet we had never seen, but who was sure to be wearing heather shades.

The second hand clothes from America that Dilys and I wore for our photograph on the balcony at Barons Court, at the time of the post war family reunion, were a shell pink knitted dress for Dilys, and a maroon and grey check woollen suit for me with a brown and white floral blouse! By some miracle they fitted.

At this time food was rationed too, and my turquoise grandmother had the following recipe for a plum pudding with no eggs.

Rock Flat Plum Pudding

1 small cup shredded suet
1 large cup brown sugar
1 large cup plain flour
2 large cups breadcrumbs
2 large cups fruit peel — spice to taste
One and a half large cups warm milk
1 teaspoon bicarbonate soda — pinch salt
1 large tablespoon treacle dissolved in milk
add soda and milk to dry ingredients

Steam for two and a half hours in basin without cloth
Serve with plain sauce to which is added 1 teacup treacle.

Adventures in post-war Malaya

On our return to Malaya, after the family had been reunited at the end of the war, loyal Chinese servants lined the quay in Singapore Harbour awaiting their returning European families. Ah Chuan had buried our family silver and when he met us again he returned it, denting the silver tray with his spade when he dug it up. My mother refused to have it mended as she said it was a historic memento.

Travelling north up Malaya in 1946 to Trengganu, where my father was to take up his post as Chief Police Officer, we were jolted about in an old army truck, sitting in the back on mattresses. The journey took several days. Once my father sat on the bananas by mistake. Our diet consisted of bananas, sailors' biscuits (like dog biscuits) and disgusting red palm oil. When Nina Dilys and I complained our mother told us that we were having an adventure! Men pulled us across on the river ferries with the use of ropes. Vehicles that had fallen into the water could be clearly seen. It was all very primitive.

When we reached Trengganu, we found it to be the most beautiful and unspoilt place we had ever seen. The heavy coconuts thudded onto the white sand which was covered with huge jellyfish. I will never forget the smell of that beach, warm and spice-laden.

One day the Sultan of Trengganu invited me to tea. I was nine, and went on my own. When I walked into the Palace I found him surrounded by his courtiers with silver kris (daggers) tucked into their gleaming cloth of gold sarongs. He showed me some of his treasures, ivory carvings etc., and when it was time for me to go home he gave me a large wooden model of an East Coast fishing boat.

We seemed to be almost the only white people in the State. One, Major Freeman, borrowed our 'car', which was an army Dodge truck, to hunt a man-eating tiger. Nina Dilys and I were later taken to see the dead tiger in a clearing in the jungle. It was then transported in our truck. For weeks afterwards the truck was infested with tiger ticks which bit us and made us itch.

Our huge great cook was said to be a pirate!

Esther Remembers Three Childhood Christmasses at Sea

Sailing on the small cargo boat *Ben Lawyers*, laden with bananas, from Malaya to England, with 12 passengers, not long after the War. My younger sister Dilys and I were the only children on board. At Christmas a great fuss was made of us, and the sailors wrote our names in white paint on the diningroom portholes. They even gave us presents. A passenger gave me a copy of *Treasure Island* which I read on this voyage when I was nearly ten, reminding me of the tales of pirates on The South China Sea, one of whom was said to be working for us as cook in Trengganu. One sailor gave me his wartime issue New Testament with a message to the Forces from King George VI.

After seeing timeless Biblical camels as we passed through the desert scenery of the Suez Canal at Christmas time, we visited the large department store Simon Artz at Port Said. The toy department was lit up by twinkling fairy lights — the first that Dilys and I had ever seen. At these Middle Eastern ports the ship was boarded by amazing Gully Gully men in red flower pot hats with black tassels, who produced yellow fluffy cheeping chicks from our ears!

Was it Christmas at Colombo when little naked brown boys dived into the murky water of the harbour to try to catch sparkling coins thrown to them by the passengers of the big liners? Although it may not have been Christmas, a sailor gave me a magnificent shining shell of mother-of-pearl and turquoise blue.

Waking up at 2 or 4 in the morning to lumpy long stockings bulging on our bunks in the little cabin aboard ship, probably somewhere in the Mediterranean. A pretty baby doll in a frilly net skirt, a tiny tin car, a book, some fruit and nuts all complete. Dilys and I both got the same.

On one of the larger ships, a passenger dressed up as Father Christmas with presents in a sack. I rightly guessed that he was dear old Doctor Black.

Balloons and coloured streamers, music, dancing and games. Feasting, laughter and wonder on the deep, seemingly endless, blue sea.

I SAW three ships come sailing in,
On Christmas Day, on Christmas Day,
I saw three ships come sailing in,
On Christmas Day in the morning.

Tanglin,
Cameron Highlands
Pahang
November 20

Dear Mummy and Daddy,

Thank you for the letter and the parcel you sent me. Last Saturday the whole school stirred the Christmas pudding and wished. This picture is of me stirring it.

Yesterday and the day before there was shooting practise; and yesterday there was a mock attack; some soldiers pretended to be bandits and tried to get in but they did not succeed, they looked awfully funny with leaves sticking all over them.

GUARDS

Thank you for the trowel, it is very useful, and my garden is coming on very well, my geranium cuttings look as if they will flower very shortly soon.

In History we are revising Tudor period, Thank you for giving me the ovaltine and jam, I have just finished both tins and they were very nice.

x x x x x Love, from Esther.

The Emergency in Malaya 1948—1960

During the Emergency — the armed struggle between the governing forces under British colonial rule, and trained Communist guerillas lurking in the jungle and trying to seize power — I was a ten year old boarder at Tanglin School in the Cameron Highlands, protected by soldiers from the Coldstream Guards and the 4th Hussars.

The education was on English lines. When I had been a pupil at the Convent in Ipoh I was taught all about Malay history, geography and maths. Here at Tanglin when it came to Christmas I was chosen to sing Gold in *We Three Kings*.

However the Emergency became too dangerous for us children to be educated in the cool air of the jungle-clad hills, so we were evacuated in a military convoy which was guarded overhead by an army plane which crashed into the roadside jungle in flames, killing all on board. I have depicted this in one of my Tiger paintings.

Tanglin School re-formed in Kuala Lumpur so I was sent to live with my Flowerdew grandparents there in order to continue my education. I flew north to Ipoh to join my parents and sisters for the school holidays. At this time I had riding lessons on ex-racehorses. I also had many swimming lessons — Oh that top board! — so much so that when I was at Headington School, later on, I won silver cups for swimming and diving.

ON HOLIDAY CONVOY

Esther was one

FIFTY two children\left the Tanglin School, Cameron Highlands this week for their summer holidays travelling the 40 mile jungle road to Tapah in armed vehicles of the Fourth Hussars.

Coldstream Guards gave roadside escort at various points on the journey. An R.A.F. Brigand which was to have escorted the convoy crashed in thick jungle about 200 yards from it.

Sunday Times special correspondent Dickson Brown and staff photographer Yong Peng Soon took these exclusive pictures.

Malayan Police Mata Matas led by Noel Nicholls

Perak   *Trengganu*

Schoolgirls Esther and Nina Dilys with guardian grandmother Margaret Nicholls

Separation and reunion

In 1951 my parents left by sea for Malaya, taking Dilys and Finola with them but leaving me behind in England. My guardian was my uncle Geoffrey White. I boarded at Headington School, Oxford, and spent the school holidays with the Whites in Warwickshire, or on the Wests farm in Norfolk. One Christmas was at a hotel with the Oakley family, when I caught pneumonia and was looked after by the Heatleys. In those days children were not flown out to join their parents abroad.

After 18 months or so my parents came home for three months' leave and we had a family camping holiday in Scotland. I did a lot of sketching when I did not have tonsillitis.

My parents then returned to Malaya taking Finola, and leaving Dilys to board at Headington with me. Our guardian was then Grandma (Margaret Nicholls). I did pencil drawings of my distant family from photos. Julianna, the baby, was born in Malaya in 1953.

Our parents' next leave was delayed because my mother had suffered a nervous breakdown. When they did finally return to England Dilys and I met one-year-old

Julianna for the first time, and a scarcely recognisable six-year-old Finola. I had to look after the family for several months while my mother was in the Warneford Hospital. This was the time I was supposed to be sitting my O Levels. I returned to school to sit the exams, and passed five subjects.

Clockwise from bottom left: Finola, Julianna (twice) and Noel

Alderminster Apples

As mentioned earlier, I remember spending school holidays at Alderminster Lodge, in Warwickshire, in a beautiful, big, white, Georgian house with a huge garden and stables. This belonged to my aunt and uncle, Christian and Geoffrey White. Their children, Alice and Jeremy, were about Nina Dilys's age. When she joined me 'at home' she also enjoyed staying with them. They had a cat called Spider, several dogs amongst them a pretty pair of King Charles spaniels called Maurice and Michael, a pony, and, at one time, a pig I remember! Also two goats called Gert and Daisy. The garden connected with the churchyard through a little gate and footpath. The primroses at Easter spilled over both ways, and the bank in the back garden that rolled down to a small river, was a golden blaze of daffodils. We had wonderful games with places to hide, in the yew trees. The only thing I didn't like about staying with the Whites was that Alice and Jeremy were frequently invited to parties and I had to stay behind. I think this was because they were parties for police children, as Geoffrey was Chief Constable of Warwickshire, and I was probably too old anyway. With my small camera I took a photograph of Alice and Jeremy picking apples at Alderminster.

Warren Hills

As a schoolgirl I spent many happy summer holidays with Oliver and Arete West on their farm Warren Hills at Oakley near Diss, Norfolk. Their magnificent Suffolk Punch cart horses, several dogs, and many cats made it a fascinating place to be young. In their garden there was a tennis court and a huge oak tree with a swing which I painted with Rachael, their six-year-old daughter on it, pigtails flying. I also painted their grown-up son Michael on his red tractor in a golden field. This picture won a prize at Headington. Then I painted Rachael, red plaits and blackberry juice around her smiling mouth.

It is nice to be settled so near 90-year-old Arete now, in our Crossingford phase. She has knitted so many tiny garments and snug pram covers for our grandchildren.

I remember my first arrival in this part of the world, when, aged 13, I arrived alone by train at Diss station and stood gazing up the seemingly endless long, straight platform at another solitary figure standing there, who turned out to be my new unknown fair-haired cousin Peter West who had been sent to meet this homeless schoolgirl. Our grandfathers had been brothers — brothers too of the famous Gordon Flowerdew VC who, as a small child, had been completely unafraid of the great Shire cart horses at Billingford Hall. It is interesting that now, just when they were in danger of becoming extinct, they are being bred again, and a pair are being broken in just up the lane from us at Crossingford.

Billingford Hall

by
Arete West

Now aged 90, Arete West writes about her childhood memories of Billingford Hall, the Flowerdew family home where my grandfather was born.

I remember so well the enormous bed, a four poster, when staying there and sleeping with Aunt Eleanor when she was home. On the way upstairs was a landing with a large clock and I have a drawing of the same by A[unt] E[leanor] done in] 1898.

Breakfast was always an ordeal for me — the maids all came in to the dining room, the cook, parlour maid, kitchen and scullery maids, the latter such a young girl. All very quiet and still. Then Granny said a prayer and read out of a large bible. (I have that family bible with the births etc. of family [recorded in it]). [I] have no memory of the food at all, but remember slipping into the kitchen and the cook always found me something tasty. She was such a dear. [I] cannot recall ever be[ing] seen, [so I] suppose [I] always chose the best time. There were large covers hanging on the wall and used when the meals were taken into the dining room and the maid going round with veg[etable]s etc to each person. [I] remember the large dairy and the scullery — the latter such a large cold place — and felt so sorry for the little girl who had all the washing up etc. to do. (All has since been pulled down and is now a garage).

[I] always seemed to be in trouble as I would be picking out tunes I'd heard, on the piano. One day to my horror [there was a] thump-thump from above and [I] knew my grandfather was very annoyed. [I] always was rather timid and frightened of him, so just up[ped] and ran out into the garden. This was when he was bedridden. A dear old nurse was there then and she used to take me with her when she went for a walk.

There was a wall dividing the garden from the field and a small road was for the carts etc. and people used to walk to church along that way. Aunt Eleanor always was sure to have hollyhocks growing there.

Christmas was such a very different event there. No presents until evening. A table and cloth stood in a corner and the presents were put under the cloth by all during the day, then in [the evening] we children took [it] in turns to take one parcel from under the cloth, take it to Granny, she then read out the name and we took it to the person. Of course, [attendance at] church was essential in [the morning] and Granny generally played for the hymns. Evenings were spent round the piano and song singing — [on] Sundays just hymns.

Granny always had her knitting bag hanging on her chair and between courses and the maid clearing the plates away, there she was knitting away. She taught me at a very early age to knit and crotchet. I had to sit still (very difficult) beside her on a little stool and to watch and copy her. A very easy and useful method that I used later in life.

When Granny went visiting, Parker always had her pony ready in her little 'tub' cart on wheels, and I used to enjoy this outing, generally down lanes and seldom met much [other traffic]. We were always made welcome at the big houses and [made] only very short visits, [to] relations generally.

Our trap was larger (two steps to get up into) and I remember going over to Billingford for Christmas, my parents in front with my sister and baby brother, and my other brother and I in the back on the floor. We had a lovely travelling rug to cover us and at night it was rather cold and the lamps were alight. We lived the other side of the river in Hoxne in one of grandfather's off farms. Of course no distance but it seemed a very long way to us.

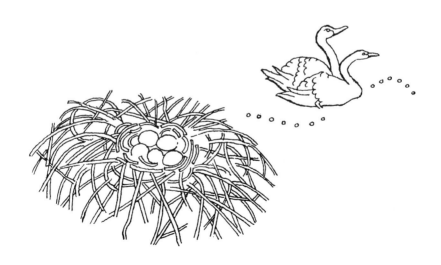

Swans' Way

After O Levels I left Headington for good, and spent the following term at the Oxford School of Art. I would have liked to have stayed on there, but Daddy had to find a job in England as the psychiatrists at the Warnford Hospital had advised him that Mummy should not return to Malaya. He found a job as Warden of the Slough Community Centre and the family moved to an old rectory in Taplow. It was a solid, Victorian, three storey house with seven bedrooms, and five doors leading to the outside world. We called it St. Nicholas' Lodge.

My parents decided that it would be a good idea if I started to earn my living, as there were little ones still in the nest. So, instead of going to a nearby art school, I went to work as an apprentice-trainee animation and background artist at an animated cartoon film studio, which occupied a large old house in Taplow. It was very interesting, and after paying my parents for my keep I used to buy traditional jazz records.

But before this happened, I should tell you about our arrival in Taplow. I had been sent on ahead to open up the huge house. Mummy was still in hospital and Daddy was supervising the move from the Oxford end. I was a bit nervous on my own in a strange place at night, not knowing a soul in the village. I was 17. My uncle, Geoffrey White, asked the local police to keep an eye on the place. Two or three days later, when Daddy was supposed to be bringing a load of small items from Oxford by car, it was very icy and he had a terrible accident. I was alone in the house at Taplow when a policeman knocked on the door and asked if I was Miss Nicholls. My heart sank. He told me that Daddy's car had skidded on the ice and he had been injured and taken to hospital in Windsor. I had to accompany the policeman to identify the one million and one little things that had been packed into the car, ranging from coat hangers and squeaky toys, to hairbrushes and shoe-laces. Then I had to go and see Daddy in hospital. He was obviously in a lot of pain and shock. Somehow we got settled into St. Nicholas' Lodge, but Daddy's leg was never better.

The house had a wonderful view over fields at the back, and some lovely old apple trees and rose bushes in the garden. The manure for the latter was brought to us by a young earl — Poly Norbury, who pushed his wheelbarrow up and down the narrow public footpath that ran alongside our garden.

At Skindles Hotel, on the River Thames at Maidenhead, a party was held when Malayan police officers, with names like Harry Harper, Claude Fenner and Micky MacNamara, met to present Daddy with a sword of honour on his retirement. It was engraved with the dates of all his appointments on the silver parts of the scabbard. After lunch at the hotel the party moved on to our house, opposite the church in Taplow, where, it being a fine summer day, we all gathered in the garden, which was looking really pretty.

I had pneumonia at Taplow, and was in bed for quite a long time. Dr. Jacques was amused by the books in my bedroom: *The Power of Personal Magnetism* was a course I had sent up for, and *Self Help* by Samuel Smiles had been given to me by my parents when they had said goodbye on leaving me behind in England when I was 12; this was supposed to help strengthen me, because it was full of tales of children who had been sent down coal mines at the age of eight and ended up by being Prime Minister or something similar, also *Pollyanna* for the same reason.

Being an artist trainee I was put to work on all the different processes involved in making an animated cartoon film, such as trace and paint, animation, and backgrounds. Cartoon film making was a very expensive process, costing thousands of pounds for one minute on the screen. This was at the time when commercial television started and needed lots of short animated advertisements. It was quite exciting, seeing one's drawings coming to life. One exercise, which I had to do, was to work out the many drawings needed to portray a parachute collapsing as it hit the ground. There was so much work involved in designing a simple movement that it was not surprising when the costs became too much and Polytechnic Studios, Taplow went bankrupt.

My parents then thought that perhaps I should go to university. I was 18. So I had to get some A Levels, and spent a very interesting two years in the Sixth Form of Slough High School, which was a grammar school for girls. I was in Herschel House.

I couldn't help observing backgrounds at Slough; while I was there mother arranged for me to be presented at Court, and curtsey to the Queen. I met some real debutantes and went to a few coming-out balls where I met many deb's delights. Mrs. Bellairs, the wife of Admiral Bellairs presented me at Court together with her two granddaughters Fiona and Lorne McKean. I became quite friendly with them.

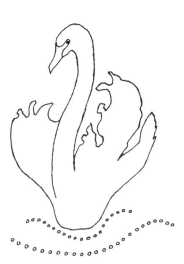

My Father Noel's Career

Copies of citations for my father's decorations

Officer of The Most Excellent Order of The British Empire

Mr. Nicholls joined the Malayan Police Force in December, 1927, and has served with distinction in both Singapore and the Federation. Since the war he has held important posts and has been Chief Police Officer, Trengganu, and later Perak, the heaviest charge in the Federation. Since March, 1950, Mr. Nicholls has been officiating in the rank of Senior Assistant Commissioner in the Criminal Investigation Department and has been intimately concerned with the re-organisation of the Department. He has worked zealously and the improvement of the work of the C.I.D. is due in no small measure to his leadership.

HM King George VI's Birthday Honours, 1952

Meritorious Service Medal from the Government Of Perak

Mr. J.N.M.A. Nicholls: His outstanding leadership and devotion to duty have been a source of inspiration to his men. He never spared himself in the discharge of his duties. It is largely due to his splendid handling of the various problems arising out of the Emergency that the war against the Communist bandits is meeting with success.

King's Police Medal

Mr. Nicholls has been Chief Police Officer in the State of Perak since September, 1947. This appointment has always carried very considerable responsibilities and the burden has been enormously increased since the outbreak of crime and banditry which led to the present state of emergency and which has existed now for more than a year.

Mr. Nicholls has shouldered his burden with courage and resource. He has produced new and practical ideas and has been receptive to and keen to implement new methods of dealing with the situation. By his hard work, leadership and knowledge he has been largely responsible for initially holding the outbreak of lawlessness and latterly for improving the security situation in the State of Perak. During the same period the expansion and reorganisation of Mr. Nicholls' Police Contingent has progressed very considerably, again largely due to his personal effort and example.

HM King George VI's New Year Honours, 1950

OBE   KPM   Perak

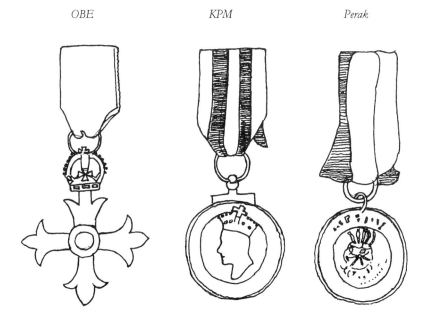

Cameronian Regiment
Scottish Rifles

John Noel Mason Ashplant Nicholls
OBE KPM

Swan's Way   Prefect's badge

Esther in London 1958

St Nicholas Lodge, Taplow 1958

The stately sailing swan
Gives out his snowy plumage to the gale,
And, arching proud his neck, with oary feet
bears forward fierce, and guards his osier-isle,
Protective of his young.

James Thomson

Swans' Way — remembered by Esther Herschel-Shorland, 1995

When all the world is young, lad,
And all the trees are green:
And every goose a swan, lad,
And every lass a queen.

Charles Kingsley

My soul is an enchanted boat,
Which, like a sleeping swan, doth float
Upon silver waves of thy sweet singing.

Shelley

With that I saw two swans of goodly hue'
Come softly swimming along the Lee:
Two fairer birds I yet did never see

Spencer

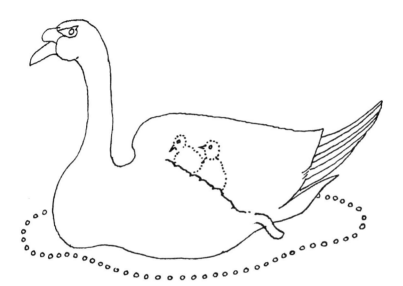

*The Lord Chamberlain is
commanded by Her Majesty to summon*
Mr and Mrs Noel Nicholls
and Miss Esther Nicholls
*to an Afternoon Presentation Party at Buckingham Palace,
on Wednesday, the 21ˢᵗ March 1956, from 3.30 to 5.30 o'clock p.m.*

*Ladies: Day Dress with Hats.
Gentlemen: Morning Dress: Non-Ceremonial Day Dress
If in possession Swords should be worn.*

Court, Courting and Marriage

Royal Command

After careful fittings for my dress — which was made by Mrs. Lunt, who sewed the ornate, full-skirted ballroom dancing team display dresses — and choosing a small matching straw hat, I had lessons in how to curtsey the right sort of curtsey before the Queen.

In the taxi driving slowly up The Mall towards Buckingham Palace, we could see other debutantes, all with unaccustomed hats on, and nervous smiles. In the Palace I found myself sitting next to a girl called Mary Wells who had been in my class at St. Pauls when we were 12. We were now 18 and 'coming out'. After making our slow deep curtseys to the Queen and the Duke of Edinburgh we were given tea with the famous Lyons chocolate cake. I felt that my dress, of pale turquoise brocade, with several layers of net lining the skirt, was more like fancy dress than the day dress decreed on the royal invitation, and Daddy did not wear his sword. In later years my daughters were to wear my gown for dressing up. It was the pride of the acting box along with the guardsman's uniform that his grandmother, Eileen, made for William when he was four.

At a coming-out ball that I was invited to, which I think was hosted by the McKeans, a cabaret was staged in the floodlit garden, with dancers from the Glyndbourne Opera Company performing in the moonlight.

In the autumn cycling through Burnham Beeches was absolutely thrilling because of the russet colouring of the stately trees.

Mummy was very good about getting us to meet local young people. There were a lot of tennis parties, which is one of the ways that John and I got to know each other. Some mutual friends called Morgan-Smith introduced our two families because we were both ex-Malayans. John's mother organised tennis parties with tea and cucumber sandwiches on the lawn in the Martin's garden in Warfield. Christopher and Angela Maycock used to come and play.

John's parents, Christopher and Eileen Shorland, lived in Warfield in a cottage-style house called Meadens which had been built by Eileen's aunt, Dorothy Herschel. The Bodleian Library has a collection of watercolour paintings by Aunt Dorothy. Christopher, retired from the Malayan Civil Service, used to go hunting every

Monday, and looked terrific in his riding gear. Eileen kept hens and was helped in the garden by her sister Carol who also lived in Warfield. Eileen was working on a history of the parish which she later published. She was a keen member of the WI especially in its acting of plays. She also enjoyed her games of bridge. John's father had been interned in Changi like my father.

My mother was so good at getting us to know young people, and giving parties for us, where there was dancing and candlelight, that our doctor's wife, Mrs. Jacques called her Mrs. Bennet as in *Pride and Prejudice*!

At Slough High School I made all the decorations for the sixth form dance, and was allowed to keep them afterwards. So for a party at St. Nicholas' Lodge I hung my homemade silver stars from the drawing room ceiling, where they turned gently and shone on the dancers below.

When I was at Mrs. Hoster's Secretarial College, John invited me out for the first time. He took me to the University College, London, Engineering Ball. Soon after this he took me on the Thames in his homemade canoe. A thunderstorm soon developed and as we sheltered under the weeping willows on the bank, he gave me his first kiss!

I had gained the Gold Medal for ballroom dancing at classes run at the Slough Community Centre where Daddy was Warden. I had learnt to glide along — but John's dancing teacher had taught him to bounce up and down — however we managed!

At Taplow I found it difficult to adjust to being just another fledgling in a newly-established nest, after having the joint adult responsibility for the family with my father in Oxford, when Mummy was in hospital for months being treated for a nervous breakdown.

I thought that as the eldest I should be giving the little ones treats. So one day I left a note for my mother telling her where we would be, and took Finola and Julianna to the cinema in Slough to see a classic Walt Disney fairy tale which I thought would be fun for them, and I was interested in it from the professional angle myself. Unfortunately I must have timed it badly because my mother came to find us, with the aid of an usherette and her torch, and was very cross.

My mother was getting much better now that she had her family all under one roof. She joined the WRVS and helped to deliver Meals on Wheels to the elderly and housebound. The sound of Mummy playing the piano, usually Chopin, wafted up the stairs to our bedrooms at night. This was lovely.

I played the piano for the Sunday School in the village.

Tony Flowerdew took me to Henley Regatta along with some of his Old Etonian friends.

Patrick Chapman took me to the Farnborough Air Show, and to meet his parents in Deal. He first proposed to me at The Dorchester when we were at a table hosted by my mother at The Victoria League Ball. I was wearing a long white dress, and the Hoskins pink topaz cross. Princess Margaret was the Guest of Honour.

After we got engaged John took me to see Observatory House in Slough. This was where his famous ancestors, the Herschels, had lived. Slough did not want to maintain the large building, and John's mother could not afford to keep it up. There was a great debate in Slough as to what was to happen to the building, which was opposite the Granada cinema. Eventually it was decided that it should be sold as a building site. This meant that it had to be demolished. Daddy, as Warden of the Slough Community Centre and Chairman of the Slough Council of Social Service, and President of the Slough Branch of the St. John's Ambulance Brigade, had some say in the matter so he did not want John and me to announce our engagement for several months until all the fuss had blown over. So we waited.

I don't know what was happening to Finola and Julianna at this time, except that they were having riding lessons on ponies, and Finola was having speech training. Finola was very good at acting, and starred in a school play as the Judge in *Toad of Toad Hall*. Julianna took up the cello although Uncle Dugald's instrument was too big for her.

For one birthday Finola was given a pedigree Skye Terrier puppy called Primrose. This was after I had more or less left home and was living at The United Societies Club in London. The dog was very highly strung and snappy. When I came home my mother advised me to flatten myself against the wall and remain quite still in the hopes that Primrose would not notice me! Skye Terriers are faithful one man dogs, such as the one in the tale of Greyfriars Bobby, in Edinburgh, but hate and mistrust everyone else it seems.

Nina (formerly known as Dilys) left Slough High School after O Levels and went to be finished at the Constance Spry School at Winkfield Place. There she learnt domestic and flower arranging skills. Nina met Sir Stanley Spencer who was painting

the portraits of the Martineau family who lived near us in Taplow, which of course is not far from his beloved Cookham and its Swan Upping.

When I had finished at Slough High School my parents did not want me to go to university after all, although Miss Crawford said that my results would get me an Exhibition to Reading University to study the History of Art. Once again 'the little ones' were given as the reason, and my father said that I must get a qualification quickly so that I could earn my own living as soon as possible, so I must do a secretarial course. I was booked into Mrs. Hoster's which, ironically, was a few doors down from the Royal College of Art, where I could see some of my old friends from the Oxford School of Art entering the doors.

When I first went to Mrs. Hoster's I played up and didn't work because I hated it so much. Then a tutor called Miss Dennant talked to me and said that my parents had spent a lot of money on the fees, so I started to work and ended up by getting a First Class Diploma. While there I did enjoy typing in time to music, mainly marches, played on the gramophone, and I wrote a poem which was noticed by Miss Graves, the sister of Robert Graves; she taught shorthand there.

It was nice being in London, and I was lucky enough to find that my mother had arranged for me to live in a girls' club in Harrington Gardens. There I shared a room with Hazel Stewart, Jo Farrell, and Jane King-Lewis. We all became great friends.

Mummy also arranged for me to have drawing lessons from a teacher who had been to The Slade. But I soon found that I was too tired to have them after a day at Mrs. Hoster's. She said that I was 'the best draughtsman she had ever taught!'

In the interval between A Levels and secretarial training I was sent to the London School of Deportment, in Knightsbridge to learn how to open a church fete, and how to get out of a sports car without showing my knickers! This was aimed at turning me into a lady in a fortnight!

Jo and I enrolled for lectures in philosophy at the London School of Economics. At the first one we learnt that 'this is a table'. That slightly put us off. Then we enrolled at evening classes in oil painting at the Chelsea School of Art. We liked that better. A still life that I painted there was later exhibited at a show by the Society of Women Artists (President Dame Laura Knight) at the Royal Institute Gallery in Piccadilly.

For as long as I was based at Taplow there were no family holidays where we could get to know each other.

Being in London meant that one could go to jazz clubs with one's friends in the evenings. But some evenings I worked as a washer-up and waitress in The Grisby — an Italian restaurant in South Kensington. I got £1 for an evening's work — that is from 6pm to 2am. I also walked around London carrying my drawings to show to the galleries, but without success.

When I finished at Mrs. Hoster's my parents told me that I must find a job quickly as my allowance would be stopped at the end of the month. Daddy really wanted me to join the police or the army but I had not got his courage. My only qualification was in shorthand and typing. I went to work at the War Office as a secretary. Soon after I joined it John and I became engaged. He was in his final year at London University studying Mechanical Engineering. I was able to type out his thesis. He got a job as soon as he got his degree, in defence work with the Brough Aircraft Company in Yorkshire. So we started our married life in Yorkshire.

We were married at St. Columba's Church of Scotland in Pont Street, London. Uncle Victor MacEchern travelled down from Scotland to help officiate at the service.

Wedding presents arrived at St. Nicholas' Lodge, the 'Heirloom' tea service from Sir Noel Mobbs, Daddy's boss, arriving by chauffeur-driven Rolls Royce.

My trousseau was made by the woman who sewed the dresses for Ballroom Dancing Championships at the Slough Community Centre. She also made my wedding dress and the bridesmaids dresses. Mummy said that I should give my younger sisters my collection of jazz and dance music to pay for my trousseau. This I did.

I was so frightened of Daddy's temper that I thought the whole thing would be called off.

We had our wedding reception at Londonderry House, Park Lane. Jack Masefield, nephew of the Poet Laureate, gave the speech for the friend of the bride but said that he didn't know me so would talk about my parents instead. No friends of the family knew me because I had been left behind in England for four years from the age of twelve. I wish that Geoffrey could have made the speech really, as I had spent such lovely school holidays at Alderminster Lodge and he was such a good uncle, and great fun.

Amongst the music at our wedding service we had *Praise My Soul The King Of Heaven* for the entry of the bride, and the choir, high up in a gallery at the back of the church, sang the anthem *God Be In My Head*. During the signing of the register we had *How Lovely Are Thy Dwellings* by Brahms.

My wedding dress, floor length, with a stiffened petticoat, was of creamy white satin, with white chiffon over the bodice and long sleeves. John's mother lent me an heirloom veil of creamy lace, which was long enough for the pageboy to hold. My jewel was the family diamond and pearl pendant that my godmother Aunt Nancy Gaffikin gave me as a wedding present.

I arranged for my bouquet of white and cream flowers to go to Grandma who was being looked after at The House of Prayer.

The six bridesmaids looked enchanting in mixed sweet pea colours. They were Claire and Prudence Shorland, Nina, Finola and Julianna Nicholls, and Alice White. They carried pink roses. The four-year-old page boy was my godson, Richard Kelvin Hughes. Rosemary Kirke from the War Office took lovely pictures of them all, especially the children. Finola was about 12 and Julianna, six. Christopher Maycock, now a doctor and later Cassie's godfather, was best man.

The wedding cake was decorated with lovers' knots and stars.

For our honeymoon we went to Annecy in the French Alps. There were lovely walks up the mountains through Autumn woods — with mysterious signs saying 'beware the Grisbi'! The hotel terrace where we often dined looked out over the lake. John took lots of photographs of boats and swans in the reeds. This was September 1959. I was 21 and John was 24. We often pedaloed to the centre of the lake where we ate the huge packed lunch provided by the hotel, and swam in the nude. On our return from our honeymoon we trained to Paris where we collected our car, a grey 1934 Riley, which we had left outside a police station. It was just as we had left it except for a sprinkling of golden autumn leaves on the roof.

The Sword of the North

This is the title of a big book compiled by my great uncle Dugald MacEchern giving details of many Highland families including ours.

When John and I lived in Yorkshire during the first year of our marriage we went on a camping holiday to Kilmelford, in Argyll where my father Noel Nicholls had been born in The Manse, and where his ashes now lie in the tiny churchyard. His mother, Margaret, had been a MacEchern before she married the Rev. John Ashplant Nicholls.

From Kilmelford we went to Oban where we boarded a boat for Iona that historic island where so many northern kings are buried. We returned to Iona with our three children many years later. How white was the sand on the beach, and how turquoise blue the sea. Students were busily working to restore the ancient cathedral.

My grandfather, John Nicholls, had been approached to see if he would go to Iona to help rebuild the Christian Community there, but for various family reasons it did not work out, and in spite of his inspired Gaelic preaching he felt that a younger man was needed.

My great grandfather, Charles MacEchern had been brought up near the home of Flora MacDonald.

John Buchan's *Book of Escapes*, and *The Prince in the Heather* by Eric Linklater, and *Napoleon and His Marshals* by AG Macdonnel tell of Neil MacEachern and his son. Neil had come from the island of South Uist. After the '45 he escaped with Prince Charles to France. It is recorded that he spoke French, English and Gaelic, and that he was a gentle, quiet man, and that he played the violin. His son became one of Napoleon's Marshals and Duke of Taronto. One of his descendants created a famous garden in Italy.

My grandmother Margaret Nicholls was a talented pianist who studied under Tobias Matthay, and then went to Hollywood where her acting gifts were much in demand. She was a great beauty and known for her charm.

John and I camped on land belonging to sheep farmer Alistair Craig who lived opposite The Manse in Kilmelford and remembered our family living there. He allowed us to establish our VW camping wagon high up in the hills above Kilmelford near an inland loch. The first time we went there as newly weds he allowed us to camp on the banks of the loch, and we walked round it finding driftwood for our camp fire. We cooked all our food on this. We had a holly green TR2 sports car then. Later when we had the van we had our three children with us. Once we parked it in a gypsy caravan park and their children tried to pick a fight with ours, calling them gingernuts because of their Titian hair. We saw the gypsies much prized Crown Derby china in the windows of their luxurious caravans.

We took our three children to Edinburgh to introduce them to Uncle Victor and Aunt Amy MacEchern. Catherine spilt her scalding hot tea on her lap and had to be plunged into a bath of icy cold water by Uncle Victor. Our three youngsters played and sang *Amazing Grace* and *The Lord is my Shepherd* to Uncle Victor and Aunt Amy. Amanda had her guitar with her.

We took the children to the Military Tattoo at Edinburgh Castle which they loved, then back to Uncle Victor and Aunt Amy for a night cap before putting the children to bed in the back of the van, and driving them all the way home to Leamington without a stop until we reached a lorry drivers' cafe for a 6am breakfast of delicious tea and sausage and eggs and toast. The children woke up for this having slept all the way from the north to Leamington Spa where we lived then.

While we were living in Yorkshire, in the early days of our marriage, John was doing defence work designing, testing and developing a method of seat ejection from naval carrier-borne aircraft and flight refuelling with the Blackburn Aircraft Company at Brough.

I attended classes at the Kingston upon Hull School of Art, doing pen and ink studies of botanical specimens. I also used to do oil paintings of the Humber Estuary.

A robin often visited our kitchen — probably for the crumbs.

My little sister Julianna, aged seven or eight, came to stay in our flat in Hessle, near Hull. I washed her long fair hair, and we took her to the seaside.

We frequently went camping for weekends on the moors. This was especially enjoyable in the spring when the tiny lambs were bounding about. It was not so enjoyable, however, when the cattle were let out after their winter confinement in close quarters, and these huge beasts galloped down the village streets intoxicated with their newfound freedom.

Crown Derby

After a year in Yorkshire, John and I moved to Derby when he got a job with Rolls Royce Nuclear Division. He was to work on nuclear submarines — still defence work.

Our three children, Amanda, Catherine (Cassie) and William were born in Derby — the girls in St. Mary's Nursing Home.

Following a visit to the Crown Derby factory, where we saw the fine bone china being made and decorated, my love of fine tea cups must have started, although I did not draw or paint a series of pictures of them until many years later when we came to live at Crossingford.

Soon after we arrived in Derby John became a Sunday School teacher taking the older girls and boys at Quarndon Church.

When my sister Nina was engaged for the first time things went wrong and she had a nervous breakdown. We took her to see the Rev. Peter Tomlinson, a relation of John's who was Rector at Repton. He and his wife were very kind and helpful and it was suggested that Nina live with us for a few months. She did this, seeing a specialist in Derby. Most of the time she baked jam tarts so we had lots of lovely tea parties to eat them up. We helped each other. I was expecting William at this time.

William was born at home, 548 Kedleston Road, with John present, in 1966, and my mother suggested that he be named Kedleston or Allestree. Our house was in Allestree, overlooking Kedleston Hall. I wanted to call him Jack but a family name was decided upon. Like all our babies William spent hours lying outside in the big black coach-built pram. When he was born, Mossy, our help, sat on the stairs and burst into tears. The midwife was called Nurse Bottomer and liked spanking little bottoms!

I went to classes at the Derby School of Art, studying portraiture.

Mossy's husband Tom Moss, designed and built a magnificent climbing frame for our children, which we have now erected at Crossingford for our grandchildren.

There was a sandpit in our garden, and several black rubber car tyres for the children to bounce on. The garden was very pretty, with lots of flowering trees, and spring bulbs. The milkman used to swing Amanda on our large farmhouse gate.

Once we shared a dinner dance at our house, with Carl and Zelda West-Meads. We also had lots of children's parties with tea laid out in our large playroom which had a picture window looking out onto our beautiful country view.

For holidays we camped in Aberdovey and in Brittany.

Our first year of having a Christmas tree, and children's parties, was 1964. Amanda came with us to the market to choose the tree. But when she saw the evergreen she turned away in disappointment saying, 'That's not a Christmas tree — it hasn't got no lights.' So when we got it home it had to be decorated straight away! Then when finally it stood in its full five feet of glory — with gilded fir cones, crystal drops from a dismantled chandelier, red, gold and blue tinsel, and multi-coloured lights — Catherine, concentrating on her first tottering steps, came over, wobbled, and clutched for support at a dangling icicle, which of course brought the whole thing down on top of her ... despite the fact that we had placed it within the seemingly secure barricade of the playpen.

Amanda finds it difficult to say Christmas, and her first shot at saying Father Christmas was, most appropriately, Father Misty.

Amanda sings *Jingle Bells*, the first verse of *Away in a Manger*, which is connected very definitely in her mind with the cardboard Nativity scene we have made together, and the Old Masters' paintings on the subject. She enjoys *Good King Wenceslas* until we get to the last line — my rendering of the swooping 'fu-u-el' worries her and she says, 'Don't cry, Mummy' and puts a comforting hand on mine when we get to that bit.

When John and I went to Nottingham for the day to do some shopping we left the children at home with Mossy, our much-loved help. On returning home we found that Mossy had baked a super apple pie, sausage rolls and raspberry tarts for us. The house was looking spotless. Amanda was happily playing ring-a-roses with Mossy's little boy Colin, and Cassie was being bathed.

If Amanda doesn't want one of us to hear what she is saying she shuts the eye nearest the person from whom the secret is to be kept: thinking, no doubt, in ostrich fashion, that if she can't see Mummy then Mummy can't hear what she is saying. Sometimes she closes both eyes and announces her intention of doing some forbidden thing, then opens them and says innocently that she is going to do something that is approved of! At other times, when she is quietly occupied in another room, she will call out 'I be good, Mummy!' This is the signal for me to rush in because invariably it means that she is just about to do something very naughty and her conscience is obviously crying out for help! Once after raiding the larder she sought me out with her ill-gotten chocolate biscuits hidden behind her back, and sidled around me so obviously concealing something that she hadn't a chance of enjoying her booty.

Once I was making some cakes and had to leave the kitchen for a moment — on returning I found Amanda feeding Cassie a mixture of flour, water and cochineal — a mixture that she was officially making for the birdies, but Cassie was eating it with every appearance of enjoyment.

The blind piano tuner came. The children were in their noisiest mood — fighting over the same toy, and shouting each other down. I removed them as far from the piano as possible, taking them upstairs, where the noise continued unabated. Ruefully the nice young man who keeps our instrument in tune reminded me that he did it 'all by ear.'

Amanda's third birthday; her first words on waking up were 'Now I am big. I will be able to reach the top of the toy cupboard.' John had made her a Wendy House which she found waiting for her when she came down to breakfast. We posted her birthday cards through the letter box and pretended to be the postman knocking on the door with her parcels. Later I prompted her, 'Now what do you say to Daddy?' Whereupon she looked up at him with a sweet smile and asked whether he liked sausages!

We left Derby when William was one, to move further south to Royal Leamington Spa because John's job with Rolls Royce demanded it. Mr. and Mrs. Moss went ahead to the new house, on Leicester Lane, and cleaned it and redecorated it so that it would be nice for us to move into. Once again there was a lovely view across open countryside.

Royal Leamington Spa 1968—1985

We moved to 22 Leicester Lane, Leamington Spa, in 1968 when Amanda was seven, Cassie five and William one. We were immediately surrounded by kind neighbours; 80 year old Mr. Avery, on one side, rushed round on our arrival, offering a meal of tinned peaches and ham. The Sewells, next door but one, with their four children offering playtime on their garden swing and over the years making firm friendships with us all. I never did tell them how their budgie flew over the garden fence when we were supposed to be looking after it — fortunately it came and sat on my shoulder when I called it, so we managed to get it back into its cage! The Greens, further up the road lent us their pram because I had given ours away in Derby, thinking William had grown out of it.

Amanda and Cassie went straight to their new school — The Kingsley School. There Amanda's 'news' items about our camping adventures, thunderstorms, floods and all, got into the school magazine and earned her some stars, and some disbelief amongst the staff.

When Cassie was eight she wrote the following school essay on 'Our House':

'Outside our house there is a climing rose, it is climing up one of the posts that is holding up the ledge over the front door. We have got a lovely veue looking into the country. I have got a patchwork quilt that Mummy made, and a big cuberd that takes up lots of spase.'

William started at Miss Bushill's Nursery School in Vicarage Road, when he was three. This gave me the opportunity to enrol at the Leamington School of Art. There I won a first prize in a drawing competition, and I was one of the part-time students who campaigned for a part-time Diploma Course in Fine Art. William in the meantime was learning his alphabet, and making friends of his own age.

For babysitting I belonged to the Warwick University wives' rota. We sat for each other and were paid in plastic tokens.

The parks in Leamington were beautiful. The Jephson Gardens opposite The Pump Rooms, were usually full of Indians in their decorative national costumes. I often took the children there to throw bread to the water birds on the large pond with its splashing fountains. There was a picturesque bandstand near the swimming baths.

There were many beautiful Georgian houses with ornate wrought ironwork on the balconies known as Leamington Lace.

When I broke my right arm I received hot spa water treatment at the Pump Rooms, and really felt cared for.

William in the bath.

William in the bath.

Our Children Entertain Us

Little Savages

William had his six-year-old classmate to stay for the night. Bath-time was much enjoyed by both:

Nicky: 'Hey Willie, sometimes I think I've got so many whiskers on my legs I think I'll grow up to be a gorilla.'

William: 'Yes, some people *do*! My Daddy nearly did.'

Snowdrops

by William age five or six

Snowdrops!
First they point up to the sky –
Then they droop down to the ground.

The Seasons

by Cassie age nine

The leaves are falling off the trees
    falling
        falling
            softly.

Next the snowflakes will be coming
    softly
        falling
            down.

After the snow has fallen down
    all white
        and covering
            everything

The sun and rain shall melt the snow
   and make
      all things
         grow green.

The summer comes next and gives
    some colour
      and
        happiness.

St Nicholas

by Amanda age 11

St. Nicholas is a gentle man,
    So good and kind and true,
He brings the children presents
    (As he used to do for you.)

He comes down through the chimney
    (On Christmas eve you know)
And fills the children's stockings
    With goodies to the toe.

The Sea

by Amanda age 14

Moaning, sighing, whispering softly
As it rises and falls in a wave-like motion,
Capturing thoughts, emotions, dreams,
Thus we are charmed by the depths of the ocean.

No-one can fathom the bottomless waters,
Yet all are intrigued by the deep dark vault,
The hungry, grasping, merciless killer
Which none can control or bring to a halt.

A tower of strength, the icy waters
Hesitate not to claim their due,

Reaping, snatching up all within reach,
Hiding all evidence far from view.

And yet, this seething foamy broil,
Which makes one's blood run cold
Bewitches us all with sweet sea music
Enshrouded with mysteries still untold.

And when the stormy tumult is over,
The calm serenity of the sea,
The gentle hush, the lull, the peace
Is a solace and friend to me.

Letter from 22 Leicester Lane, Leamington Spa
17 December 1970

Dear Eileen and Christopher,

This may be our Christmas letter as we are getting pretty near the date.

Unfortunately I missed the girls' school Carol Service due to a wretched cold. However John managed to get time off from work to go and watch Catherine in the Nativity Play (not a camel this time!) and listen to Amanda read the First Lesson.

Yesterday I went to watch Catherine's ballet class — Mums being invited to sit-in as it was the end of term. It was interesting to see them do their leg and arm exercises, party polka, character steps, dance and mime. They certainly had to work very hard but obviously enjoyed it — all the terms were in French, and in their green brief tunics it gave an impression of a pretty thorough and authentic grounding in the elements of ballet. Catherine was a lot smaller than the others, and with her Titian hair neatly up in a chignon and back from her face with a white hair-band she really did look quite long-necked and ballerina-like. This and drawing and painting seem to be her best means of expression.

William was very excited when he broke up because he had such a lot of things to bring home to show us, and in the top of the carrier bag his teacher had put a balloon. Patting this balloon high into the air occupied him happily for two whole days — until it hit a sharp projection. He wept for it as though for a lost companion but Catherine pointed out, 'You can't expect your balloon to live forever.'

On one occasion when I had been sitting down and trying to find a moment's peace with a cup of tea and the newspaper, William batted his balloon particularly hard across the room and it landed on me. I was rather annoyed. William quietly picked the balloon up, and turning away from me said to it, 'Bounce politely!'

Amanda wrote:

> Christmas is a happy time,
> When all the bells in Church do chime,
> The Christmas star all shining bright,
> Guides us all home through the night.

Catherine wrote:

> There is a little Christmas tree,
> Bright and green,
> With all its little ornaments
> Shining bright.
> O lovely little Christmas tree
> Sparkling bright.

and so from all of us to all of you much love and many kind thoughts this Christmas and always,

Esther

York Road School of Art, Leamington Spa

Thoughts on a Pile of Cardboard Boxes
Autumn 1970

Cubic – inaccurate.
Triangular angular linear shadows interlock lighter shapes
Bulging slightly or slightly concave.
Wobbling stack of overlapping empty boxes.
Individually tilted but the balance of the whole is maintained.

Purpose of units? For holding things – hollow,
Light in weight, silent to handle, shuffle – muffled thud.
Straw or shavings for packing objects in the boxes.
Small hard heavy wooden balls packed therein.
Smaller similar balls in glass container.

Lack of colour of the glass merges with the white background.
Almost the tiny balls seem suspended in the air.
Top surface of projecting right box shines and reflects
But the glass sparkles.
All other boxes, tissue, shavings being completely mat.

Feel the tissue paper is soft and crinkly,
The glass is like a bubble – delicate vase-vessel like a chalice.

There is variety in the shape of the boxes.
Some yawning wide – gaping towards the light.
Some squat, comfortable.
Others narrow restrictive confining
But all are turning their emptiness towards the light.

The structure rises like a child's tower of building bricks –
Or opened boxes stacked neatly at the side of the room
At the end of Christmas Day. Happy Boxes!
Discharged of their treasures (tins of pheasant and Christmas pud.
Boxes of dates and dolls prams, and newly knitted ponchos).

Or waiting boxes, placidly patiently waiting to be filled
And restacked – pushed tossed and shoved.

They are still and empty now.
Not new as they have served one purpose at least already.

White background, grey shadow – no colour?
Colours of mud, brown paper, string, glue,
Sawdust, coconut matting,
Mushrooms, Khaki, desert.

The boxes are smooth, lightweight,
Bendable, crushable, kickable,
Or a bed for a puppy –
A carpenters workbench,
Glint of glass,
Empty removal van –
Bonfire.

Esther's meditation above helped with a painting that was bought by Dr Pat Carpenter and her drawing of the boxes won First Prize in a drawing competition at Leamington Spa.

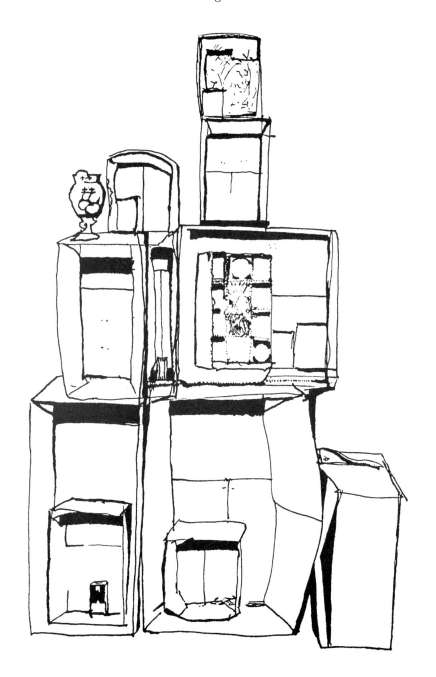

On Sketching the Ruins and Gravestones Kenilworth, May 1971

The light sky dips between the trees
touching the gravestones.
I sketch, ... stretch, ... freeze!
The sun shines on the stones and grass
the waving weeds and mown path
But not on me.
The hollow where I sit and draw
between the fallen ruined walls
is shaded, windy, bleak and raw
with peoples litter on the floor.
A dead bird lay there the first day.
Now the grass is turned to hay
The tall white lacy graceful weeds
Sway – delicate and fairy-like
among the solid speckled crosses.
The fresh green grass shoots spear and spike
upwards sharp and spark with dew.
The lump of ruined pink stone pile
leans and rests behind the rail
to keep exploring children out.
The ruins press down to the ground.
But upward outward all around
The fresh spring growth is flourishing
Frothing top bush brush the sky!
Cold and coffee-hungry I
Seek the cosy sanctuary
and the talk and company
the warmth and baking smells!
Then linger longer than necessary
before returning again alone
Stalking and reading the names on stone.
Back to the hollow – the grass and the sky
The branches and tangle of twigs and leaves
The darkness of shapes against brightness of light
The texture and colour and pattern – and flight
of a bird disturbed from her nest
where a hole in a ruin gives shelter and rest.
Crumbling monuments man has left
weathered and beaten; yet pretty and bridal in
white spring blossom carnival garlanded.

This is a peaceful place today.
Silent gravestones old and grey
All around sweet beauty keeps
renewing yearly while they sleep
beneath this complex chain reaction.

A cross is such a simple shape
But associations make
Us aware
of human drama everywhere
Before these states which we see here
This end and this beginning
These ruins and this spring.

Esther

Letter from Amanda at a Discoverer's Camp in Swansea when she was nine

I am having a lovely time. When I got here Mr. Westcote said that there was a postcard for me. It was from you. We went to the seaside yesterday. There were lots of lovely rocks, and a lot of huge waves. Once there was a very big wave and Bridget and I were sucked out. We struck a rock and I cut my foot. We both were under water for ages and we both thought we would drown.

Last night I did not get to sleep until midnight because all the girls who were 10 and over kept on giggling and talking. Mrs. Westcote kept coming in to tell them off. She came in for the last time at one o'clock. I was asleep but I woke up with all her shouting. She said that she would call the police. This morning she said that 6 people would have to go home tomorrow because they were so naughty. Bridget was lucky because her mother gave her some disprins to take at night to help her get to sleep. My lilo has a leak.

Mr. Westcote asked me to read the lesson today. In about 5 minutes we are going to have a meeting. I had to borrow Bridget's Bible because mine is too old fashioned.

I forgot to say that last night everyone was eating sweets and crisps, except the Ashleys and Bridget and I. Give my love to Roddy, Polly, Granpins, Granpops, Catherine and William. Everyone says I am very brown. Mrs. Westcote said to me 'Are you a boy or a girl?' I said I was a girl. I also give you lots of love. On Tuesday we are going to see the caves and we are going to climb a mountain. I am afraid that Bridget and I seem to be catching a Birmingham accent because every person except the Ashleys, Bridget, a boy called Adrian and I comes from Birmingham and there are 23 children.

John was going abroad on business a lot now. He was sent by Rolls Royce to China, South America, North America, Canada, Germany, France, Italy, Spain, Algeria, Japan, Bangladesh, Holland, Finland, Denmark, Sweden and Norway. He always brought back lovely presents for us all, costume dolls for the girls, wooden fishing boats for William, and perfume for me.

At about this time I had a one-man show of my paintings at the Art School at York Road. The Birchleys, friends of John's at Rolls Royce bought a painting of doves on a rooftop with autumn leaves, and the mathematician at Warwick University, Professor Rourke, bought a picture of red and black squares with postcards inset of a shell, a woman in red, and the Cutty Sark. Those pictures went for under £10 each.

The pre-war 1930s-built house on Leicester Lane, while having a lovely garden, with a woodland corner where we planted bluebells and our children made dens, with four bedrooms was too small for us. So we decided to move to 5 Vicarage Road which was a six bedroom solid semidetached Edwardian house with attractive fireplaces and large windows looking across the road to the beautiful Old Vicarage where the eye surgeon, Norman Brown, lived with his pretty wife Wilga and their three children. They lived under a stately beech tree that looked handsome all the year round. The Rev. Jo Humble lived in the modern vicarage next to it. And Mr. Meanley, the bank manager, was our attached neighbour. The Murray girls, straight out of Jane Austen, lived next door on the other side. They were very glamorous and good fun. We called them The Marigolds. When I broke my arm they passed home-made casseroles and pies over the garden wall for us, until I was able to cook again.

For three years running John's parents, Eileen and Christopher Shorland, accompanied us to Italy where we camped together under the shade-giving pines. In the evening Eileen read to us about the sights we saw in Florence, Siena, Pisa and Ravenna and Venice from H.V. Morton's *A Traveller in Italy*. The camp sites always had swimming pools and as we walked around the camps at night we could hear the crickets chirping noisily.

We also camped many times at St. Davids, the New Forest, and Brecon Beacons. Seven pilgrimages to St. Davids were said to be equal to one to Rome.

During this time there was a lot of musical activity in the family. Amanda was Head Chorister in the alto section of the Holy Trinity Church Choir. She had violin lessons on her Sanctus Seraphin, and piano lessons. Cassie had ballet lessons, and for a while learnt the oboe until she could no longer bear its sound. William was in his school choir, at Arnold Lodge, which was associated with the RSCM and took its medal tests.

William got up at 6 o'clock every morning to practise the piano. His earlier attempts to learn the violin with Mr. Polyblank ended in tears.

When Finola came to stay we took her to the romantic gardens at Hidcote — straight out of *Sleeping Beauty*. Finola was very interested in gardening at that time.

When the French exchange girl Stephanie came to stay we took her to the grand old house at Charlcote, where Shakespeare is said to have poached the deer in the park.

Another place we liked to take visitors to was Snowshill Manor in The Cotswolds. We used to go to the theatre at Stratford a lot.

When I was 36, and we had been at Vicarage Road for a year, I had a nervous breakdown. Amanda was about 11, Cassie 10 and William seven. John was working abroad a lot. I was helping with the Holy Trinity Church Stewardship Campaign, and studying for a Fine Art Diploma, part-time, but suddenly it all went out of focus and I was full of fear. My thoughts were a nonsense. My friends put me to bed and summoned our GP who called a psychiatrist to come and see me. John was told about it at work and was aghast, but when he got used to it he was a tower of strength.

It took a few years for me to get over it. I felt very lethargic and depressed and put on a lot of weight so felt unattractive too.

The Rev Michael Mansbridge advised me to read Proust and take the time to rest without feeling guilty about it. The Rev Cyril Yuall told me to read Psalm 91. My Quaker friend Peggy Watkin brought her knitting and said nothing.

For the next few years I walked to the hospital, walked to the schools, the library and the shops. John very gallantly went to Sainsbury's once a week for our needs. I did not feel like going to art school, but managed to cook the evening meal and look after the family. During this time the children took their important exams. Amanda married Clive, Cassie went to the Art School to do the Foundation Course. William went from Arnold Lodge to Rugby School. William sat the Scholarship to Rugby, and did sufficiently well to be exempted from the Common Entrance Exam.

When William was at Rugby doing his O Levels his appendix burst and he had to be admitted to hospital in the middle of the night. This meant that he could not sit all his exams, but he was able to get into Newcastle University on his A Level results.

Rugby was taking girls in the Sixth Form by now, and William managed to acquire a girl friend called Elinor Booth who was very clever and attractive and got a scholarship to Girton. Her father worked for Shell in Japan and her parents gave William a wonderful holiday over there. While there he taught English to Japanese businessmen, played tennis with the Crown Prince, and was entertained by the members of the William Herschel Society of Japan.

In the meantime Cassie got a place to study Interior Design and Three Dimensional Design in Brighton, ending up with a First Class Honours Degree.

Amanda went into nursing and began writing articles for the nursing magazines. Her husband Clive Garrett was a policeman but gave it up. He tried various things but what he really wanted to do was hill walking.

John played the flute with various friends, and I accompanied them on the piano. He also learnt to play Real Tennis and enjoyed it very much.

Then the day came, which John had foreseen, when Rolls Royce forced him to take voluntary redundancy. He decided on a complete career change and wanted to get away from the Midlands.

At the same time my parents, Noel and Wendy Nicholls, were finding Crossingford too big for them and wanted to sell it so we bought it. The stress of this time caused John to lose consciousness one night and he was hurriedly admitted into hospital where he spent two or three days in intensive care. However he recovered, and we came to live in Norfolk.

Christmas at Vicarage Road

Number 5 Vicarage Road, Lillington, Leamington Spa, had two rooms below ground. This cellar regularly flooded and was dark. One day we decided to have it properly dried out. The Marigolds next door had a sweetly-scented flood in their cellar which we assumed was their fragrant draining bath water. We wanted to make use of our underground rooms — for William's train layout in one room, and John's workbench in the other. When we whitewashed the cellar, with the children's enthusiastic help, the new space looked so much like monks' cells that we decided to hold our own ceremony of carols down there. The warm golden glow of nightlights made the bare whitewashed walls look more beautiful than ever. For the Cellar Service each member of the family read a Lesson and we all sang some carols, and the children also played their recorders. So our first Christmas in our new home dawned with light and music.

William sang in the Arnold Lodge Choir at the School Carol Service every year. One year he was chosen to sing the opening solo in *Once in Royal David's City* but he had a cold so couldn't undertake to do it! Some of the fathers were asked to sing in the choir too so Peter Briggs and John did their bit.

We took Nicholas Cadbury with William to see the Royal Tournament in London when they were both aged about eight, and we all had a scrumptious tea in Harrow with Nina and Francis and gorgeous baby Bella on the way home. This may not have been at Christmas.

After John's mother died his father Christopher and sister Prudence used to come to us for Christmas. Also Melissa Henney spent several Christmases with us when her parents were sailing around the world.

One Christmas we took our children to see the Royal Ballet perform *The Nutcracker* at the Festival Hall. The snow scenes were magical.

Plum Pudding Cooks

Two little girls and one little boy
Wanted to play but not with a toy.
They decided as Christmas was drawing near
That it would be grand to help Mother dear
By making a pudding of everything nice
Including some brandy and sugar and spice.
Plum pudding so round and steaming so hot
Would crown Christmas dinner (with crackers – the lot)
And secret additions to the pudding would be
The silvery charms and thimble you'd see.
So William and Cassie and likewise Amanda
Rolled up their sleeves and had a bonanza.
This very good time enjoyed by us all
Resulted in having a seasonal ball.
The fun which we shared with friends and relations
Who came to join our home's celebrations:
It's easy to make and delight to consume –
The tradition continues in our dining room.
So try out the recipe's crystallised crumbs
And leave some for Santa whenever he comes.

We wish you a Merry Christmas and a Happy New Year from John & Esther. Amanda Catherine & William.

Cassie at the piano

William at Vicarage Road playing the mouth organ

Thistle Make You Whistle !

The MacEcherns were bards and tellers of tales — here are a few family jokes:

Fire

told by my Great Uncle Victor, the Rev CVA MacEchern MA, FSA Scot

When the Hotel in Aringour in Coll was burned to the ground I had the misfortune to be away on the mainland on holiday.

When I returned and looked upon the blackened ruin I expressed my real regret at having missed the excitement of the conflagration. It was not that I wished the hotel to have perished, but merely that if it had to be, my witnessing it could not have done it any harm.

The first big fire I remember was the Inverness Music Hall in Union Street. Our home was in a flat adjoining the Hall and at midnight we were all roused out of bed fearing that our own house would soon be ablaze. Father out on the street was so excited that he scarcely knew what he was saying. Suddenly the great roof caved in with a mighty crash. At the same time the firemaster, Mr. Treasurer, was instructing his men to play their hoses on the minister's house windows. Father was heard addressing him in these words: 'It's going very well. Isn't it, firemaster?'

Christian's joke

The MacEcherns are a sept of the Macdonalds who are, or who think themselves to be, the tops in Scotland.

An elderly Miss Macdonald was browsing amidst the wonderful statuary on Iona, admiring one of the Virgin with a Macdonald inscription underneath, exclaimed 'My, I never knew the Virgin Mary was a Macdonald.'

The Wrong Boat

by Victor MacEchern

(This actually happened to my brother when minister of Lochranza)

To Rothsay pier one Saturday
There came a young Divine,
To catch his boat for Arran's Isle,
But he cut it rather fine.

I saw him bravely sprinting
As the steamer moved away,
He leapt across the gunwale
And alighted quite O.K.

'A splendid jump,' the Captain cried,
'To you I raise my hat;
Olympic stars could scarce exceed
A flying leap like that.'

'I simply had to catch the boat
Or Arran folk would find
There wouldn't be a sermon preached,
If I were left behind.'

A light lit up the Captain's face,
'Your leap is a fiasco,
This boat is not for Arran bound,
We're making straight for Glasgow!'

Prunes

The big joke — always told by my father Noel Nicholls, at Crossingford mealtimes when he was master of the house, and we used to bring our three children over for Easter and Christmas celebrations — was the story of the prunes that he refused to eat when he was a little boy. Once he went to bed with his prunes uneaten, but during the night there was a terrible thunderstorm. Fearfully he crept down in the dark and finished up the unwanted dish muttering to himself, while looking up at the dark sky lit with glaring lightning flashes, 'All this fuss about a few prunes!'

Letter to the
Rev CVA and Mrs MacEchern

from Vicarage Road Christmas 1975

Dear Uncle Victor and Aunt Amy,

We still remember with pleasure our visit to you in Edinburgh. Here, instead of a Christmas card is some news of our family doings: Starting with the eldest, Amanda, now fourteen, is working for her Grade 7 piano, and Grade 5 violin. Her ambition is to become either a Doctor or a Music Teacher. We have just bought her a lovely violin made in 1945 by a Venetian with the inspiring name of Sanctus Seraphin. Amanda is deputy head chorister of the Altos in the Holy Trinity Church Girls' Choir, and is singing in the chorus of the Pirates of Penzance which her school is producing in conjunction with the Boys' College. Her piano teacher composed and dedicated a piece to Amanda entitled 'Thoughts in Deep Red.' I feel that I should paint a reciprocal picture for her with the same title. The following is a poem by Amanda that appeared in her school magazine last term:

Spring in Jephson Gardens

Walking through the dreary streets
All I see is dull and grey.
What season is it? Who can tell?
The shops don't change their drab array.
Concrete pavements, tarmac roads,
Bustling shoppers, roaring traffic,
Movement, noise and rushing bodies,
Who knows where or what we are?
But walking through the giant gateway,
Wrought of iron, rusty, old,
All the grime, the noise, the traffic
Melt away to sun-kissed flowers.

Jephson Gardens: a cool, deep pond,
Dainty fountains, sparkling and fresh,
Fluffy ducklings, snowy swans,
A massive carpet of tinted blooms
Composed of every shade and hue,

A fresh, sweet dew, the blazing sun,
Singing birds, chirping gaily,
Gliding swans, displaying their grace.
The atmosphere is gay and bright.
No dull pavements or smoke-filled air,
But sweet aromas of budding flowers,
And a cool fresh breeze. It's spring once more.

Catherine, thirteen this December, passed her Grade 3 Oboe after two terms, but then gave it up because she could not bear the noise! She is now learning the classical guitar. She has insisted on having her lovely golden hair cut short as she was tired of having to plait it for school. She has bought herself an old hand-sewing machine. This summer she and William attended the Cycling Proficiency Training Course for Schoolchildren run by the Police. In the Test at the end of the course William failed, even though, or perhaps because, he had a new bicycle for the occasion (!) and Catherine came top with 99% and has now been invited to compete in a cyclist-of-the-year competition. She is artistic, and always making things, but wants a career where she can help people and is thinking of Occupational Therapy. She plays netball and hockey for the school. Here is one of her limericks:

There was a proud man of Bengal
Who always said 'Pride after fall.'
When they said 'Are you sure?'
He replied 'Ever more.'
Then he went and tripped up in the hall!

and Catherine's poem about a snail:

The snail, he is so quiet and slow
His silver trail in the moon will glow.
Gradually and slowly he will move.
He goes along his trail so smooth.
He goes straight on in the dark alone.

The cruel thrush follows his way
For the poor little snail he will betray.
He snatches the thing up in his beak.
And crushes the snail that's so small and weak.
He scatters the poor thing's shell around,
Like broken china it falls to the ground.

Lastly Catherine's poem on pigs:

Pigs aren't really dirty creatures
Though people say they are.
Though they have some ugly features
They're probably cleaner than you by far.

You might think pigs are very rude.
And lie in the mud all day.
But if you were a pig, I bet you'd
Do exactly the same as they.

William, aged nine, played cricket for the school in the under nine-and-a-half team this summer, and I enjoyed the spectator's privilege of home-made-cakes and dainty sandwiches and tea in the pavilion with the team. (One of the incentives for being in the team being the super tea). William also sings in the school choir and was the first boy of his age group to earn his pale blue Junior Singing Boy of the Royal School of Church Music ribbon and medallion. His great interest at school is Geography, and he has been fascinated by the television series on The Explorers.

William wrote the following two limericks:

I bought a pair of glasses
With frames of different grasses
I saw very well
Till they fell down a well
And that was the end of them.

There was a young man from Porthclais
Who lost an egg and spoon race.
His family were sad
But his neighbours were glad
And now he lives in disgrace.

John has been a tower of strength as I have been recovering from my nervous breakdown during the last eighteen months. He has just become a Life Member of the National Trust so we hope to visit some interesting places soon. We camped near St. Davids again this summer, and enjoyed a concert in the Cathedral. We sailed our dinghy and the children fished happily for hours. Amanda saw an eighteen inch long fish swim past her line and was so excited that she threw herself into the sea after it.

John has taken to printing his own coloured photographs. From time to time he has a bit of trouble with his ulcer otherwise he is keeping fit. This year we have been enjoying the vegetables he is growing in his little patch at the end of the lawn. There is just enough grass to play badminton on. It is a very small garden but walled which makes it private and sheltered.

I am painting with our Post Diploma Group, and studying colour harmony. I am very interested in the work of Vermeer, and of Fra Angelico (having been most impressed by the latter on a visit to the Convent of San Marco in Florence several years ago). I have been asked to paint a picture for our Church, and one for my psychiatrist. At a recent concert I noticed that a Rachmaninoff piano concerto is dedicated to his psychiatrist!

We thought of you both at the christening of Dilys' baby Isabel in the crypt of St. Paul's Cathedral, and wished that you could have been at the family gathering. The baby looked very beautiful in a lace gown that Dilys bought in Sicily.

We all send you many loving thoughts for Christmas
and the New Year

Esther

Summer Holidays at St Davids – 1992

Camping on the farm – it's National Trust
Children play with dog and ball and raise the dust.
But there is mud upon the simple track –
A far cry from the motorway that takes us back
Across all Britain to the Norfolk scene
Where we'll remember holidays that once have been.
It is a pilgrimage we often make
For pleasure now and for long old time's sake.
The rain is unrelenting on a cold grey day.
Next morn dawns bright with cloudless sky – hooray!
To end with fiery sunset flaming round the hills.
The moon full over water silver spills
To make a path for mermaids' flashing tails –
This is a land of dragons – windy Wales!

Amanda longed to adopt the kitten at the farm in Garlic Street

Poem based on *Desiderata*

by Amanda Herschel-Shorland

It is a rash and noisy world
Full of lusty greed and war.
Too many secrets are unfurled,
Too many keys unlock each door.

Peace in silence you'll always find,
Though psychology truth's revealed,
For the deepest corners of your mind
Are forever from the daylight sealed.

Always willingly listen to others,
Even those illiterate and poor,
They want an equal hearing, brothers,
Don't treat them as dirt upon the floor.

Be friendly and kind,
Be strong in your soul.
In love and friendship pow'r you'll find,
Work hard and well to fill your role.

God to us all a gift has endowed,
It remains for us to improve in return,
Those who compare them get bitter and proud
And jealousy, vanity their weak heads turn.

Never scorn or mock or cheat,
Watch out for trickery and grudge,
For 'though many an honest chap you'll meet,
A downright bad'un's hard to budge.

Be yourself, don't pretend or act,
Be honest and truthful, don't deceive,
Use your discretion and some tact,
And that which doesn't concern you, leave.

Love is lasting, it's light never fades,
Don't be sarcastic about it or its ways,
And although affection has many shades
Love shines forth forever with unnumbered days.

Do not rebel against changing time,
Give up your youth with grace and goodwill,
For we're safely guarded by God sublime,
Who, despite our bad ways does love us still.

Don't be depressed by imagined fears,
Which may arise when you're lonely or tired,
Be strong in spirit, and over the years
You'll find the happiness in you admired.

Everything has a right to live,
You no less than the birds and bees,
Make the most of this blessing, and ask God to give
A joyful heart and a mind at ease.

What e'er and who e'er you see God to be
Worship Him, love Him, His commandments obey,
Beg His forgiveness on bended knee,
He'll reward you well on Judgement day.

And despite all the sorrow hate and despair
This wonderful world is still full of beauty,
So strive to be happy, be strong and take care,
Enjoy life, love God and perform well your duty.

Flowerdew News Ancient & Modern From Ruth

December 1983   Vol. 5 No.4

Snippets

Perhaps not quite the right heading for information on William Herschel, the discoverer of Uranus. He was first a professional musician an accomplished performer who composed much organ music as well as concertos and over twenty symphonies. After his great discovery he was given a royal pension — in 1782 — and thereafter was able to devote himself to astronomy.

Why William Herschel in the Flowerdew A & M? From him is descended John Herschel-Shorland who married Christian Esther Flowerdew Nicholls, eldest daughter of Noel Nicholls and his wife Wendy Flowerdew. At the Golden Wedding celebration in Oxford of Douglas and Sheila Flowerdew, Wendy, John, Esther and William were all present. William Herschel-Shorland, as well as his father John, played in the Family Cricket Match that day. Seven Flowerdews played, one umpired and another scored. Of the twenty six people (yes twenty six) who played cricket that day the remainder were Flowerdew relatives plus three girl friends. A total of forty seven, all related in some way, attended the celebrations.

Letter from schoolgirl Amanda at Holiday Camp

Dear Mummy and Daddy,

We arrived here safely at about 2.20p.m. and had a cup of tea, we were then issued with our gear — Waterproofs, (which are miles too big and drown me) and wallopping great clodhoppers. I look a fool because I am wearing size 8. At first the man who gave them to me thought I was teasing because I'm not particularly tall, and he didn't see my feet! We then went for a walk in the 'back garden' which is a steep mountain-hill.

Our instructor is Dave Hoarly (or something like that). After our walk during which Dave told us about the rocks (limestone) we had a shower and another cup of tea and a slice of stale cake.

We were then free for the rest of the evening, from 5.30 - 6.30 it is now 6.00 at 6.30 we will assemble in the dining room for supper.

We sleep in Dormitories of 4 except one where there are 8. I am with Claire, Yvonne and Nicola.

Bye now, the bell's just rung for supper.

Hello again, I'm now digesting a meal of tinned grapefruit, beefburger, chips, peas, and apple pie and custard. Yum.

At 7.30 we've got a lecture on something, I'll tell you what when we've had it!

It is now 9.15 and the lecture was on Mountain Safety. Tomorrow (Tuesday) we are going rock climbing -Proper rock climbing with ropes and helmets! Later this week we shall be going down lead mines, climbing mountains, camping in a mountain hut, walking, swimming and having films and lectures on these outdoor activities. We shall be doing all these things in our groups of 8.

In the evening we can sit in the common room and listen to records, write letters, or read etc. Alternatively there is table tennis,(but you have to buy your own ball), snooker and a football game (which costs 5p).

Ah, they've just brought in more tea and biscuits they seem to love serving up tea in this place.

With lots of love from Amanda   xxxxxxxx

Letter from Cassie studying in Brighton

Dear Mum,

How is the house, your silk flowers are no doubt coming into their element now, or are there lots of Michaelmas daisies to fill the rooms with?

If you come down to Brighton I shall have to show you round 'The Lanes' which is an area in the centre of Brighton orientated towards rich tourists, very 'Covent Garden Marketish' but fascinating to walk round. There are shops full of ball gowns, expensive antique shops, toy shops etc. Heaven for window shopping — I shall only ever look round on Sundays I think (when shops are closed and no temptation).

It was lovely this Sunday, it having poured all Saturday, the sun was out and I cycled down to the sea front, it is an amazing sight, green deckchairs, Navy Band, candy floss, rock, changing huts etc.

Have you been thinking about the trunk room, or even got into action? Don't forget to look into the middle drawer of the large cupboard/shelves where the lace and fans are. Maybe you would take some appropriate action about their preservation.

I am having a go at Christmas card designs for lino-cuts — have I already mentioned it? Will Finola be at Vicarage Road for Christmas?

There is a pub in Brighton where Jazz bands play regularly and they serve food. It is a bit of a Brighton Poly meeting place but I'm sure you would love it.

I am enjoying the marmalade and the lemon curd is delicious!

I must go - too much to do. With much love and always thinking of you. Cassie x

Letter from Sheila Lomas, the daily treasure, at 5 Vicarage Road, Lillington, Leamington Spa.

Dear Esther,

Thank you for your last letter. Over Christmas we had the rabbit die so I bought one last weekend I fell in love with it, at the pet shop.

Are you having a holiday this year, Karen and Nick are talking about hiring a caravan they say well Mum why dont I go but I would rather stay at home. I think you like going away Esther, this summer I am going to buy a set of chairs and a table for the back garden.

It is nearly a year since you have moved it has gone so quickly I used to love your back garden. You have planted some fruit trees so that will be nice when you get your own fruit. I have put some Blackberrys in the bottom of our garden. They were from the Allotments by me they have built all houses on the ground by Pound Lane. I hope your family is well also your Mum and Dad.

My sister is waiting to see if she has to go into Hospital about 4 years ago she had an operation on her legs for ulsers but the ulsers came straight back but now she is in terrible pain all the time.

Do you remember I had an operation the same year for my ulsers, I hope that my sister will go back and see if they can heel them.

I hope William is doing well at Newcastle also Cassie at Brighton I must bring this letter to a close please give my regards to all the family
       Love
         Sheila

Sheila made us some beautiful crepe paper roses for our Silver Wedding. When we left Leamington she knitted me a lovely Aran cardigan as a surprise, and gave us a tape of Scottish songs. She had lots of pets who were much loved and usually came to violent ends. Her own visits to hospital were recounted in gory detail. She was a 'Lollipop Lady' at the local school crossing for 25 years.

Esther with broken arm at Crossingford with John

Crossingford Lodge

In 1985 we moved to Crossingford Lodge, Doctor's Lane, Pulham St. Mary, near Diss, Norfolk. John did a lot to the house: plastering, painting, plumbing, wiring, and I helped by doing a lot of the painting, and altering our old curtains to fit.

The following year John enrolled to do a Teaching Diploma at the University of East Anglia. Thus William and John were both at university at the same time, John for the second time round.

I studied at Jenny Goater's kitchen class at Palgrave. She had taught Art at Millfield, and was clever at suggesting new techniques that were fun to try.

Then I met Nelly van der Zwan and we struck up a painting partnership. We met once a week in each other's houses in order to draw and paint together. This was a very fruitful collaboration and lasted for several years until Nelly had to return to Holland. Now as I write this I am told that there is a good chance she may be coming back to the village to live in her former home The Grange. This is probably the biggest house in the village and very gracious, though during the last few years it has stood empty and been occupied by squatters. When we worked together we started by doing still lives and flowers, then in 1988 we spent one whole year doing portraits of Pulham People. Altogether we each did about 30 portraits in this series. I gave copies of mine to the Village Archives.

John soon joined the Pulham Village Orchestra, and after a year or two he was elected Chairman. My mother played the viola in the orchestra until she was 81.

When my parents had lived at Crossingford they had owned two ferocious Skye terriers that scared off everyone and everything. After they had gone the wild life started to seek the sanctuary of the garden and paddock, and the birds came to be fed. Now we have pheasants, moorhens, magpies, jays, different sorts of woodpeckers, wood pigeons, blue tits, robins, blackbirds etc., and, of course, squirrels and rabbits (!)

One day when I was hurrying down the lane I stumbled over some loose stones and fell, breaking my left arm, dislocating it at the elbow. It was agony. I called John, who was gardening, but he did not hear me. It resulted in having that arm in plaster for several weeks, but it was not as bad as when I broke my right arm, because I was still able to do things such as paint.

Crossingford is surrounded by fields, and after enjoying the golden corn for several summers our young decided to hold a Golden Harvest Party. But that year the farmer planted black beans so the harvest fields were black not golden! However nobody seemed to mind and a good time was had by all.

I had no help in the house for our first few years at Crossingford, but eventually Mrs Pearce, who helped my mother, was free to come and help us too.

In my father's last illness, Mrs Pearce and many kind neighbours and friends came to Stewards House, where my parents now lived, and a rota of care was formed to look after him, presided over by my Aunt Christian. I took our blue checked kitchen curtain material to hem by hand while sitting with him. Later I heard him telling my mother that he liked me sitting with him because I was quiet. Though Finola must have surprised and delighted him when she brought several fluffy yellow goslings to his bedside!

When my father was ill my mother kept up her piano teaching but this normality may have been reassuring to him.

Christian has written to tell me 'I didn't realise till much later that your father from the word go, always had the top appointments for his age and rank in the F.M.S.P. (KL, Johore, Intelligence in S'Pore, CPO Perak in the Emergency, which Geoffrey always said was a War.) As a direct result of which, again in Geoffrey's view, he was pipped at the post for the final hurdle — Commissioner — by so much younger a man, a common practice in war conditions. So, well-earned and widely expected, the loss must have been a fearful blow.'

After his retraining John got a job teaching maths and physics at sixth form level at Costessey High School and Earlham Sixth Form College. The staff there were always friendly and charming so John was very happy there.

He retired when he was 60 and we celebrated by having a big lunch party, and by going on holiday to Malaysia. John was born in Singapore in 1935, and I had spent an impressionable part of my childhood there and in Malaya, so it was a nostalgic trip for us both, as described in my travel diary Jalan Jalan.

Part of our pleasure in living near the Norfolk Broads is time spent pottering around our mooring at Hardley Dyke and sailing our boat on The Broads. Seeing the baby ducklings and tiny moorhens, elegant swans, grebes, herons, geese etc.

There is no sign of the fish in the pond that John created here, but as a heron visited it several times recently we think he may have taken them. I do love to see the heron, however, because he is so prehistoric with his huge grey flapping wings, and his long gangly legs.

Our Home

My parents bought Crossingford Lodge in 1970 when it was a romantic wreck and they had to get a lot of work done on it. In 1985 we bought it from them, when John was made redundant from Rolls Royce, and we did a lot more work on it ourselves.

When we first saw Crossingford
The holes in walls were plugged with board
And some were merely gaping wide
Giving a view of the wreck inside.

New walls were needed here and more
Windows and here and there a door.
Electricity had to be brought
And it all caused much anxious thought.

The well was filled to make it safe
Leaving the pump the yard to grace.
It was a brave romantic thing
To save the place and make it sing.

A generation on we ask
If we can carry on the task.
So we have been aplanting trees
And making bathrooms if you please.

The kitchen sink we had to move
Plastering, plumbing, wiring too.
The whole place needed quite a bashing
But its good to hang up washing

In the windy country air.
So we do not feel despair.
It's worth the effort every bit
To see the view from where we sit.

Amanda in her uniform as nursing Sister

Letter from Saudi Arabia 1986

When Amanda's first marriage failed she went out to Saudi Arabia to nurse for a year.

I've just come back from a weekend at the Red Sea. It was such a fantastic experience that there is no way a description in writing can do it justice. However, I'll try and tell you about it as best I can:- Ten of us set off in a minibus from the Hospital Recreation Centre — 8 single females and 1 married couple to chaperone us (and the husband to drive, of course), according to the laws of ! We had to have a letter of release from the hospital allowing us to leave Tabuk (another Saudi regulation!) — and this was checked by the military coast guard 3 times over the weekend!

The drive down to the beach at Duba took about 3 hours along a long, straight road. The scenery as we crossed the desert was amazing — we saw mountains rising up out of miles and miles of sand, and much, much more including wrecked cars abandoned in the sand by the roadside. (Hopefully not concealing too many dead bodies!!) At Duba we left the road for a rough track across the desert down to the Red Sea. This was a hair-raising ride really only suitable for a 4-wheel drive Jeep or Land Rover, and the minibus nearly toppled over a few times as we jolted up and down over the uneven ground which was both sandy and rocky. We also got stuck in soft sand and had to be towed out by the coast guards. We eventually reached the beach and set up camp. This merely consisted of unrolling our beach mats on the sand and erecting a makeshift tarpaulin shelter from the scorching sun.......Now it was into the sea to cool off as the sweat was pouring off us, literally! We struggled to wade across the coral reef in our plimsolls, swimsuits and T-shirts (protection from both sun and the coral). The coral was slippery, uneven and full of deep treacherous holes down to the ocean bed!! At the edge of the coral reef the water was a clear, brilliant blue, and suddenly very, very deep. We jumped/swam/crawled/fell off the edge of the reef into the deep blue sea, without much style, I'm afraid! We all had snorkels and masks to look at the ocean life and the coral — it was beautiful, breathtaking, amazing, ... such colours I've never ever seen before.

Beautiful tropical fish, in brilliant tones of blue, green, yellow, black, and rugged coral in red, blue, white — all colours in fact. It was like floating inside a huge tropical fish tank — only much, much, much more beautiful, I could not believe it in fact. It made being here worthwhile after all and I can't wait to go again. The sea was warm and so salty that we just floated — no need to swim or tread water. It was so relaxing just floating there, absorbing the beauty of the ocean life, watching the fish swim in and out of the coral. A paradise in fact.

We watched the sunset and the sunrise — over the sea at night and over the desert in the morning — it was a beautiful and romantic scene. We walked along the beach collecting sea urchins and shells and soaking up the sun and the beautiful views. At night we had a camp-fire and slept out in the open air on the sand under a clear, starry sky — the whole week-end was simply amazing and so relaxing but unfortunately it had to end and I'm back at work now. I hope to go again next month, however.

I did take some photos — but it was risky and the Saudi coast guard caught 2 of the girls with cameras, took the cameras, then gave them back with a warning that we must not take photos and if caught again we would lose not only the film but the camera as well! They are very strict about photography, which of course is illegal over here, and any photos I have taken are taken quickly and discreetly. I hope they come out O.K.

Glad to hear Mishak is still sitting on the mat and being beautiful.

Amanda

Belinda at Crossingford

The yellow flower of early spring
A daffodil to make hearts sing!
It grows in clumps beneath the trees
Our visitors from town to please.
'It must be Easter soon' they say,
'The month to follow will be May.
How lovely England is just now.'
Soon bursts the blossom on the bough.
Another winter we've survived
In spite of ice and fog. Surprised
By spring's sweet heart that always thrills
And blesses us with daffodils.

CEFN

When William was at Newcastle University he shared a house with other students. One of them was Belinda Edwards who became a frequent visitor to Crossingford.

Norman Heatley

The following speech was delivered by the Public Orator in a Congregation held on Saturday, 20 October 1990, in presenting for the first Honorary Degree of Doctor of Medicine in the history of Oxford University

Dr Norman Heatley OBE

Honorary Fellow of Lincoln College

Our honorand is a man who is well known for his modesty and kindness. He is also a scientific pioneer who is especially worthy to receive the first Honorary Doctorate of Medicine in Oxford University. Fifty years ago, when our country was threatened by deadly enemies, a tiny unit of Oxford men won a signal victory over many diseases. In this victory Dr Norman Heatley played a large part. At that time he was chosen by Professor Howard Florey to be a member of the famous team of scientists whose task was to produce in Oxford and test and investigate penicillin, or moulds. We all know that they went on to use it successfully for the treatment of patients in Oxford hospitals.

Dr. Heatley's ingenuity in extracting and purifying this substance was extraordinary. He was experienced both in improvisation and in the art of micro-engineering. He invented a mechanical device for filtering penicillin, and also devised a method of obtaining it called 'back-extraction' — from water and back into water — and a means of assaying the strength of penicillin by placing small cylinders of it on a metal plate filled with streptococci. It is not well known that this precious and effective drug was for some time manufactured here in bedpans piled up in the animal house of the Dun School of Pathology.

Dr. Heatley then accompanied Florey when he went to America to seek the help of drug companies there. Our honorand showed particular skill in communicating his knowledge of the methods of producing penicillin. He remained in the United States for some time until the Americans were manufacturing a large amount of the drug.

In short, during the war years that group of Oxford men laid the foundations of the science of antibiotics, which is now vigorously pursued throughout the world. For several decades an army of scientists, including Dr. Heatley, has engaged in testing, improving, and enlarging the discoveries made then. It is fitting that these discoveries should be celebrated at this time by a symposium held in Oxford. That period was indeed legendary: not only were our armed forces heroic figures; so also were those Oxford scientists who saved the lives of countless people. It is remarkable how much is owed by so many to these few scientists.

I present a modern Hercules, averter of evil, Norman George Heatley OBE, Honorary Fellow of Lincoln College, for the Honorary Degree of Doctor of Medicine.

This speech was delivered in Latin. Norman is related to the Flowerdews through the Symonds family. He and his wife Mercy showed much kindness to me when my parents were abroad during my schooldays.

Norman and Mercy Heatley

Sketches of members of the Pulham Village Orchestra

The Pulham Village Orchestra was founded in 1985 to give amateur players, under the directorship of a professional conductor, a wide experience of music making.

Rehearsals take place fortnightly and concerts are given, mainly in the beautiful country churches round and about to help them with their fund raising. John, who plays the flute and the piccolo, is Chairman and the committee meetings are held at Crossingford Lodge. I help with the tea, and with the art work for publicity.

Broads Mooring

We keep our boat at Hardley Dyke near Loddon on the Norfolk Broads. One day when we went to go sailing on *Dimbola* we found her high and dry having slipped her mooring on an unduly high tide. Andy, John, and Cassie and the rest of our crew had a bit of a struggle getting her back into the water. John thought of an engineer's way of doing it.

Cassie's bedroom at Crossingford

Cassie's room at Crossingford – 1991

The yellow room
Dispels the gloom
Of stressful living.
A teddy bear
A carved armchair
Great comfort giving.

A patchwork bed
Some dried flower head
An ornate fan.
A length of lace
Sir John's old face.
The carpet plain.

A black brimmed hat
To match our cat
The silly Gilly.
Some well-bound books.
The mirror looks
At rose and lily.

Old wooden beams.
The curtain seems
The Tree of Life.
A butterfly's wing
Some other small thing
Preserved so safe.

A chest of drawers
A coach and horse
A poster too.
Some white kid gloves
A view of doves
And heard cuckoo.

A box of scent
From heaven meant
To stir the sense:
Awaits a maid
Who far has strayed
...some future tense...

A book of Prayer
And hanging there
Some beads and bangles.
Two antique dolls,
Some folderols
And winking spangles.

A fountain pen
Makes this a den
For letter writing.
A desk is there
With comfy chair
And lamp for lighting.

Cassie and Melissa at 5 Vicarage Road

To Melissa

Thank you for your Christmas gift
Of pictures black and white.
Their beauty gives our hearts a lift
And make a lovely sight.

Thank you too for being host
And having Cassie there –
The memory she will cherish most
When she returns back here.

We are glad you soon will come
To see us once again.
We'll see you in the summer sun
When cricket spans the green.

Till then keep going brave and true
And as you read this rhyme –
The card is to remind dear you
Of once upon a time.

Melissa Henney was at Kingsley School, Leamington Spa, with Cassie. When Melissa's parents set forth to sail around the world on their specially built boat *Suka Hati* (*Happy Heart* in Malay) they arranged for us to have Melissa for Christmasses etc., when she couldn't join them on the boat. And they invited us to crew with them in the Mediterranean. William and Cassie particularly benefited from this. Then when Melissa was working in America as a physiotherapist Cassie stayed with her there, on her journey around the world.

To Cassie
as she nears the end of her World Tour 1992

(to the tune of *Bill Bailey* New Orleans style)

Won't you come home sweet lady?
Won't you come home?
You've been a long time gone.
We'll do the cooking baby
(You can wash it up!)
We know you can't stay long.

How have you changed sweet lady?
How have you changed?
You've been a long time gone.
Come back real soon – and
Teach us your tune –
We'll sing a welcome song!

The Welcome Party

On 26th April, 1992, a Welcome Party was held to greet Cassie Herschel-Shorland, home from her adventurous journey around the world, and to welcome Amanda and Andy's first child Georgina Crofts into the family. Prudence, John's sister, and her boyfriend Jeffrey very kindly lent their house in Kew for the occasion so as to make it easier for all the family to meet for lunch.

William's friend Bev Straw, who is on the Directors' catering staff at Sothebys, did all the food for us, concentrating on finger food from recipes collected from all around the world. Joan Ells, John's childhood guardian, provided the champagne that helped to make it all go with a swing.

In John's speech proposing a toast to welcome Cassie back he remembered how she seemed to have disappeared without trace in Outer Mongolia. She answered this with an amusing anecdote about posting cards when travelling on the Trans-Siberian Express. When her toast was proposed Georgina responded with her first audible coo.

My teenage nieces, Bella and Rosie Pagan, looking very Italian in dark clothes, dark makeup and dark hair and lots of rings on their fingers, brought a great deal of their art work for me to see.

Dear Francis Pagan kissing and hugging everyone in a flush of family feeling, was so delighted that at last a member of the family (Cassie) had been to Ulan Bator the capital of Mongolia.

Nina Pagan, whose herb farm has just been re-inspected by the BBC with a view to making another programme about it, told us in her rich operatic tones that daughter Bella had made and decorated the ornate chocolate cake that was too jewel-like to cut.

Cousin Hamish Ramsay gave Bella sound advice on how to become a solicitor.

Wendy Nicholls, mother, grandmother and great-grandmother of so many present, was recovering from a fall the night before at the entrance to the Greek Restaurant where we had supper, and was incredibly brave and uncomplaining.

Aunt Betty Shorland was observed to be sitting on the precious photograph album of Cassie's travels, which was balanced on a little table. It looked uncomfortable as well as unsafe so a chair was speedily brought. As she left Aunt Betty told Wendy that she was looking forward to having piano lessons with her.

Bev presented the food most imaginatively and artistically in large straw baskets garnished with leaves and fresh spring flowers. The decorations, as well as the food, were on a round-the-world theme, with small globes dotted about and a large map marked to show Cassie's route. There were also colourful flags from many nations and at the centre of the white lace cloth on the extended dining table there was a blue and white willow pattern dish from Billingford Hall, lent by Arete West, filled with moss and dotted with pansy heads and sprigs of forget-me-nots and fir cones and sea-shells to represent Cassie's progress by land and sea.

At an opportune moment Nina and the rest of the Nicholls clan withdrew into the morning room for Nina to be presented with her 50th Birthday present which was a combined gift from her siblings and mother. She was delighted with the 1930s' paste brooch which she had asked for, and Cassie showed her how to work the clasp that converted it into two separate twinkling clips. She told us she has a black velvet dress for it to sparkle on.

Then back into the dining room where the pink and white candles were lit on the birthday cake that Mrs. Pearce had made for Nina and which was swiftly devoured by all.

Cassie's souvenirs and sketch books from her travels were on show for guests to examine. She wore dragon earrings that she had bought in a Chinese market, a Thai silk blouse that she made herself, and a most unusual and stunning pair of trousers that she had bought in Thailand. Everyone else looked elegant in pretty dresses and smart suits.

The weather was not good enough for people to linger in Prudence and Jeffrey's beautiful garden but their lovely house held us all in a true welcome.

Letters from Cassie in Australia

6th March 1994

This week has been full socially as well as work-wise; A Private View of work, at the Caulfield Town Hall, by an Aboriginal artist whose illustrated story book I sent Georgina for her birthday; the first night teaching for the Melbourne School of Millinery; An evening drink, in a lively district of the city where clothes, flower and jewellry shops are open as late as the cafes and wine-bars, catching up with someone I know from my previous Australia visit as well as her recent time in London studying costume design; An invitation to attend a ball last night, with half-an hours notice to prepare mentally and physically for the black tie and many variations on "the little-black dress," unfortunately as is too often the case these days, loud music obliterated any opportunity of conversation, however it was delightful to look across from the dance-floor of the sailing club, thru' the masts and out to St. Kilda Bay with ship lights on the horizon. The ceiling and columns were bedecked with large polystyrene cut-out sea horses and papier maché fish all painted jolly colours.

Today, on my way into the Craft Centre I walked thru' part of the Victoria Market. There in a shop selling Australian-made goods a beautiful bowl shone out as being suitable for William and Sara. Blue inside, filled with reversed-out stars in off-white ceramic, the size of a large salad-fruit bowl. I would eventually like to produce a piece of stained-glass as a wedding gift but I wonder whether to give them this bowl as a useful interim?

16th May 1994

As I catch up with correspondence after the wedding and travels it is confirmed to me what a fine family and circle of friends I belong to. Also how important such magnificent gatherings are. How lucky we are that you provide such a base at Crossingford Lodge.

I have just written to Muffy, who I enjoyed talking to at the wedding and hope to remain closer in touch with. I have followed-up to Christian and Alice who were very much mother and daughter on this occasion.

I returned safely to Melbourne to become immediately ensconced in design work for the forthcoming Shakespeare plays as well as resuming my role at the Craft Centre and teaching.

16th May 1994

The enclosed colour photos were given to me in America by the friends of Melissa's for whom I painted a mural in 1992 with Colin, then 9 years, who painted all the creatures in the landscape. The family are currently building themselves a house out in the countryside near Utica, New York State. Melissa and I visited while I was there recently. Coyotes can be seen around the house at night. I have been commissioned to paint them a new mural with Colin on my return route back to Britain.

The black and white photo is the joy of bed-time story reading for Orlanda, Torby and myself. I hope also to enclose a few wedding/Crossingford snaps too.

I hold a magnificent image in my mind still of the tigers in the Crossingford Lodge studio. Melissa loved her card and even before opening it announced that the Blake poem was one of her favourites... She swooned over your own poem Mum...

It should be good to have the Astridges back in Britain now. Meanwhile Claire Flexen and her friend the tea book illustrator, leave for South East Asia and Australia at the end of this month. I look forward to seeing them here.

24th May 1994

Tonight the wind is strong, the moon full and the yellow leaves are being swept off their trees into the air.

The drawing of Norman and Mercy is just as I always envisage them.

7th June 1994

Enclosed is another Herschel mention. This time summing him up as an artist. I am currently interested in discovering more about colour and came across this reference in a rather high-theorising book on the subject.

Today there was a Japanese flautist at the Craft Centre. His tunes were haunting and filled the vast space as he wandered amongst the exhibits. I have also enclosed a copy of the Craft Centre news for your interest. The article I submitted is towards the end.

I have just enrolled on a computer aided design course at the Royal Melbourne Institute of Technology. Another of the steps in my aim to make myself more reliably employable in the future it is an evening course for interior designers, architects and those using design in industry.

It appears that women of my age are becoming concerned at their increasingly single status internationally, see enclosed article on this from an Australian newspaper.

10th June 1994

Last night was the opening evening of the play for which I was set designer. The costume designer was the old friend I told you about in a previous letter. The audience enjoyed it and the evening was rounded off with champagne, eats and gentle jazz music.

Cassie in Australia 1994

Esther in Australia 1940

Esther's letters from Crossingford to Cassie in Australia

January 1994

Not a real live scented bunch of flowers for you from Crossingford this time — but colourful flowers on cup watercolours to welcome you to Australia. I am actually writing this before you have even said "goodbye" to us but that is because I want it to greet you on your arrival so that you never feel too far from us!

Christian is at the moment cruising up the Nile. I wish I had put into the Welcome Party description how Christian had looked like a fierce and glamorous tiger in her stunning black and yellow outfit with her white hair tinted amber and her tawny eyes!

In his Christmas thank you letter to us Edward Cleland wrote on a V&A tiger card. Quite a jolly little one.

7th February 1994

Thank you so much for your two recent postcards depicting two appropriate pictures — as always! What a fine welcome you had with stars and fireworks.

I am proceeding brighter, lighter but Dad says 'not politer — more of a blighter!' as a result of chiropractor sessions.

On Saturday we took the big van out for a run to Walberswick. It was very misty but the bare trees and fields with ploughing looked lovely. We walked along the seashore, and Dad picked up one stone to keep and I gathered one shell. We had some beer in a fisherman's pub with photos of fishermen in days gone by on the walls.

We have bought a dear little bluetits nesting box and Dad has nailed it to a tree where it can be seen from the church view windows, but out of the way of the cats we hope.

I have now painted five large tigers but would like to aim to do nine as I think they would look rather striking hung together somewhere like St. Gregory's. When I was a child of ten the beautiful cool colonial house we lived in was in Tiger Lane, Ipoh, Perak, Malaya. It had uninterrupted views across the golf course to the distant blue jungle clad hills. Earlier when we had lived in Trengannu my father lent our truck for a tiger hunt and we children were taken into the jungle to see the kill.

The Chiropractor asked me how I get my ideas and why I wanted to paint a tiger. I told her that it was a memory. The next day in The Times I read about the latest exhibition in the Tate Gallery in Liverpool, where 'art-lovers are paying £1 to queue up and see — nothing. ...Visitors are transported from the ground floor, via the goods lift, to the fourth floor of the warehouse, where they can observe the empty room ... The whole work is entitled *mnene* — the Greek word for memory.'

16th February 1994

When we went to London, at the weekend, it was blizzard conditions. We had lunch at the Royal Society (homemade soup and garlic bread with a warming glass of red wine). Then we walked to the Royal Academy where we had coffee in the Friend's Room and saw the Modigliani drawings. In the evening Prudence and Jeffrey took us out to a Chinese Restaurant for a meal to celebrate Prudence's birthday. The Restaurant was celebrating the Chinese New Year and St. Valentine's Day all at once so everywhere were paper lanterns, flowers and streamers. When we left we were presented with red-wrapped heart-shaped chocolates.

Prudence and Jeffrey showed us their Malaysian photos. They said that there are no longer any tigers there, and little hope of reintroducing them because there have been such inroads into the jungle that they would not have enough territory. Prudence said that she had a lot of jet lag on her return.

29th February 1994

William is now 28 — and I think he has grown a bit too! He and Sara were happily sorting out the flowers for the church and the music for the Wedding Service with help from local people whom I co-ordinate to meet them at the right time and place, and then I fade into the background and let them get on with it.

Dad's PVO concert on Sunday evening at St. Gregory's went well.

In The Times on February 19th there was an article in which Deborah Moggach relived the night out with her partner of ten years The Times cartoonist Mel Calman, on which he died: in which she says what a lot of difference little things made to her that night — such as the fact that the cup of tea that was brought to her in her state of shock was in a pretty china cup. She writes: 'At St. Thomas' Hospital they whisked him away and put me in a room equipped with Kleenex, plastic flowers and a free phone. They put you somewhere alone, so you need see nobody. The extremely nice Sister gave me tea — real tea-pot, rose-patterned china. It mattered terribly. A Styrofoam cup would have been so tawdry, so disposable. Such details aren't trivial; these small acts of tact make a huge difference. A doctor came in and told me Mel had died ...At the beginning one drinks cups of tea ...'

7th March 1994

There was an excellent article about Bridget Riley in last weekend's The Times. I will put it in your room as it is a bit bulky to post and you will soon be here! It says 'Once she had found her way forward as a painter, Riley knew that she was unlikely to commit herself to a conventional relationship, let alone have a family. "I could see no place for it. It's very simple. Time. It wasn't a difficult choice. Something had to go".' And it ends: 'This process of looking sounds mechanical, a form of optic aerobics, but it is invigorating for other reasons. These paintings are like a secret garden, which you enter only after passing through a series of antechambers. Once there, you experience a profound sense of well-being. When Bridget Riley said that "to distract from anxiety through looking was important, and that distraction is neither a superficial nor shallow thing", I didn't really know what she meant. Now I do.' (by Ginny Dougary, The Times Mag. March 5th '94.

The primroses are out in the wild parts of the garden ... daffodils too. We are not yet certain whether the heron has taken all our fish.

The day after the wedding Sara is organising a Sunday Lunch for immediate members of the family — you of course are invited. This coming weekend the Stannards are coming to consult with the Marquee man and caterers, and Brian Betts re parking etc. So there will be much making of lists and drinking of cups of tea.

Mrs. Pearce is very excited about having the whole of the house nice for the wedding guests to explore. She keeps disappearing ... once I found her spring-cleaning under the top room bed (where surely no one will look?) and on another occasion she was discovered shut into the airing cupboard where she was happily folding and refolding all the towels.

We went to Church on Sunday morning when the Bans of William and Sara's forthcoming marriage were read out by Monty for the first time of asking. It was a

Communion Service — towards the end there was a terrible rumbling noise and I thought the whole place was going to blow up. But it turned out afterwards that it was the tea-urn in readiness for coffee and biscuits for the congregation after the service. It was a friendly gathering. Several people asked if it was our son who is getting married.

I must leave some space for Dad's more practical messages — Dad says he must finish pruning the roses so he just sends lots of love. So I will try and squeeze in some lines from Carpenter's Lake of Beauty.

'And the antelope shall descend to drink, and to gaze at his reflected image, and the lion to quench his thirst and Love himself shall come and bend over, and catch his own likeness in you.'

15th March 1994

Thank you so much for the surrealist Waltraud Reiner hat card for Mothering Sunday. It is most original as are her other sophisticated cards that have been arriving here.

There are now eight tiger pictures standing guard in the studio. I hope to do one more. Then they can hang in three vertical groups of three.

On Thursday Dad and I are going to the Theatre Royal in Norwich to see Penelope Keith in a comedy. The publicity shows her reclining on a tiger skin rug!

In the garden two early trees are covered in a smothering of pink blossom. Most of the daffodils are out, as are the primroses. Dad hopes that the magnolia will be out for the wedding. We don't know what the tulips are going to do yet but they are showing green.

In the field between us and the church there strides a new and commanding scarecrow. Dad says that all it needs is a hat!

Last weekend we had an invasion of Stannards and helpers to discuss all the arrangements for the wedding reception. The marquee people measured up the garden and paddock, the catering women inspected the Aga and cold storage facilities. Sara's father kept us all under control and chaired the meeting tactfully but firmly. He is very nice (Head of Maths at a comprehensive in Ipswich). We also found it easy to discuss things with Sara's mother (an artist and musician as well as Educational

Welfare Officer). Farmer Betts wife Bridget came to discuss the parking which is the only thing that may cause problems. Dad and William walked up to Mr. Pearce's cottage to ask if guests could put cars up his drive where there is a lot of space. All they found, however, was a dead mallard hanging up — no dogs and no Mr. Pearce so they will have to try again. Sara's father didn't want them to have a horse and carriage, in case it bolted, so they have sensibly booked the local white Jaguar instead.

Glad your social life is beginning to blossom. The Yacht Club Ball must have been lovely.

22nd March 1994

Dad collected your aquamarine earrings from James Tillet yesterday. There was no more money to pay. They look exquisitely beautiful so I hope you will enjoy wearing them.

The theatre was not terribly good, but the tiger skin rug was handsome, and Penelope Keith spent most of the time affectedly eating red roses!

Mrs. Pearce is now on her final countdown to the wedding. She has washed all the radiators and skirting boards.

There has been another article on hats in the paper so I will keep that for you, and hope that your work in that field is prospering. I don't know what you are planning to wear on your head at the wedding but wish you would show off your glorious hair!

27th March 1994

This week we are quietly gearing ourselves up towards Easter. We hope the tigers we sent you will arrive in time. Mrs. Pearce is making a large chocolate cake for Crossingford — with little coloured Easter eggs round the top. There is a larger egg for Georgina.

The fashion parades of wedding garments and excited phone calls across the country have revealed the fact that both Granpins and Christian have bought themselves smart rust-coloured suits for the occasion. Christian has offered to step down and wear navy. Amanda is wearing navy — there surely aren't enough colours to go round!

The other day Andy got a piece of metal in his eye and Amanda had to take him to the hospital. She had Georgina with her of course. The door of the room where Andy was being treated was left open. Amanda and Georgina could see when Andy slumped into a faint after his local injection in the eye. Georgina explained to Amanda 'Daddy gone sleep!'

Mrs. Pearce will be celebrating her Sixtieth Birthday on 26th April. I have suggested to Granpins that she and I join together to give Mrs. Pearce something that will make her life a little easier. We thought of a slow-burning cooker but she has already got one.

Dad is working very hard on the garden and it is looking wonderful. He is thinking of putting some more gravel on the drive.

Thank you for your kind offer of help for the Big Day. Some help might be needed with the flowers, and you could drive round to Arete to collect some pretty foliage — she is postponing pruning her shrubs until after the event.

5th April 1994

We hope you had a Happy Easter. When Georgina allowed us a brief respite in which to consider phoning you we worked it out that Australia would be fast asleep in bed so we decided not to disturb you. Amanda and Andy brought most of the contents of their kitchen and helped a lot with the preparation of meals. Andy made the most delicious profiteroles we have ever tasted. We all went to church on Easter Sunday. Georgina had to be carried out twice but soon returned. The flowers in church were arranged beautifully by Mrs. Chapman who was trying out some of the ideas that Sara had suggested for the wedding — trailing ivy etc. to make the flowers go further. William and Sara spent a lot of the weekend painting the pale pink walls of the conservatory. It looks much better now — no more cracks to be seen. The dolls house has been put in the top room. Dad and Andy spent a lot of Easter assembling the climbing frame. Young wedding guests will enjoy it.

Next weekend William is having his stag celebration and has invited Dad and Sara's father to join him and his ushers and best man on a hired black Thames barge sailing up and down the coast.

trailing clouds of glory...

Georgina Crofts in her soft rusty pink bridesmaid's dress
after Will and Sara's wedding, April 1994

William and Sara were married in Pulham St Mary in April 1994

Sara's father gave the Stannard family a fright last week by passing out and turning blue. I should think that having two daughters' weddings in such close proximity must have contributed towards his collapse.

Granpins has announced that she will be wearing a whole new set of underwear for the wedding!

In the study we have arranged a display of family wedding photos including those of Sara's sister and parents. These might provide a talking point.

At the weekend Georgina and I enjoyed looking at the children's art book that I bought at the Royal Academy shop. The pages that Georgina liked best were the plain deep blue end papers. She kept stroking these slowly and saying 'blooooooo', 'blooooooo.'

I took Georgina for a walk round the garden and paddock to see if we could find a rabbit. We couldn't see a rabbit but found a hole in the ground where we thought he might live. Georgina loved playing with the gravel on the drive and putting it into an ice-cream carton. Do you remember doing that at Meadens?

We can't believe that you will soon be on your way from Australia and that you will be here at Crossingford for William and Sara's wedding. Selamat Jalan!

17th May 1994

We hope you returned to your Australian base without any problems. We are really pleased that you were able to complete the Herschel-Shorland family gathering for your brother's wedding. You looked stunning in pale blue.

Dad encloses something for your attention. Having spent the first weekend after the wedding rodding out the drains because he could not get hold of anyone to do it, Dad is rather tired. We had to cancel our weekend on the North Norfolk coast because I had a cold and was in bed with lemons and honey. However we have booked for a weekend in June.

Norman and Mercy have invited us to their Golden Wedding Party. Guests have been encouraged to submit memories and comments on the Heatley partnership. We are contributing a lot of little memories of the many times they have been kind to us.

Georgina as bridesmaid by the rockery

'... so few and such morning songs ...'
Fern Hill   Dylan Thomas

*Esther wore an Isabel Auker jacket in peacock colours
at Will and Sara's wedding in April 1994*

End May 1994

Wedding snaps from different cameras are beginning to trickle in. It is interesting to see the various styles. Malcolm's are very sensitive and artistic ... Nobby's more amusing with an understandable tendency to concentrate on the Newcastle University set. There are some good ones of you by both Malcolm and Nobby. Christian caught the Nicholls contingent who managed to evade the official photographer altogether. I want to do a series of small ink and watercolour pictures of the youngest bridesmaid — in my present post-wedding euphoria I am contemplating mounting them in white lace!

Mrs. Pearce was helping at a Jumble Sale and came back with two pairs of red dungarees which she washed and ironed and brought here for Georgina. I posted the smaller pair to her, and Amanda let her open the parcel which she did to cries of 'New dungees!'

We have the prettiest pair of turtle doves, which are smaller than the wood pigeons. They like to sit on the garden bench by the pond.

8th June 1994

Thank you so much for the beautiful photos which fill certain gaps in our records of a great day. We have ordered an official photographer's portrait of William and Sara outside the church for you, and are glad that Malcolm has sent you some as well. We are still in the throes of digesting our memories of the celebration, and are so glad that the whole weekend made a glowing rounded dance with family and friends appearing, bowing, smiling and vanishing with happy sounds. Only Charlotte Dunkerley got lost and missed the service but managed to find the reception.

Charlotte arranged for William and Sara to go and have dinner with her Annie and Mike. Mike is a Major so their two year old Hilary is being brought up rather differently to Georgina. For Hilary it is a strict but reassuring regime of early bedtime etc. By the way I love the black and white photo of you reading a bedtime story to Torby and Orlanda. What beautiful children they are!

I have decided that too many of the friends I have made since we moved to Crossingford have gone to live abroad. Margot in France, Nelly in Holland, and Tricia in Zimbabwe. I miss them all! They are such interesting people. I met a lovely woman the other day at a Sunday drinks party in Tricia and Colin's marquee the day after their daughters marriage to an American. The daughter will be living in New York but Tricia doesn't mind as she is so international. Anyway, this woman is a Doctor, and a member of the Irish Senate and her hobby is buying pictures (!) but she lives in Dublin!

The scent of the honeysuckle as we walk past it in the garden is wonderful. Also an overpowering scent of orange blossom comes from the white flowered bush in the hedge near the vegetable garden.

Andy has taken Georgina to a Circus. Apparently she sat completely still entranced for two hours. Amanda says we must all take her to a Pantomime at Christmas.

Sara is investigating possibilities for retraining and going into one of the caring professions. She wants to be able to devote more time to William, but these caring professions can be pretty draining. Dad comes home exhausted from teaching, and has to take his holidays with the crowds. He is looking forward to out of season trips when he retires next year.

You asked about anniversaries and celebrations this year. Granpins will be eighty on 20th October. We may have a family gathering here for her when you return in November.

14th June 1994

Summer at last seems to be here. On Sunday Dad and I went on the boat. We saw a family of ducks crossing the river — proud parents and at least sixteen little ones all brown except for one which was yellow and looked like a chick but was swimming bravely with the rest. One of the boats on our mooring was broken into. It was Dad's turn to do Boat Watch so this was reported to him. Nothing was taken but some damage done. Dad allowed me to take three photos of the mooring.

The poppies fringing the fields are a bright sight. I stopped the car and photographed the edge of a ditch that was blazing with blue, purple, yellow and of course poppy red. Perhaps the farmers no longer spray at the edges.

Yesterday in the garden I saw a large moorhen on the pond, counted five little fish and the giant orph, saw a huge cock pheasant stalking about, and blackbirds nesting in our wisteria. Dad has put some pots of scarlet geraniums by the sundial which makes the terrace look continental.

The weekend after our North Norfolk trip Mary and Geoff Mesney are coming to lunch. They are having a weekend break nearby — actually staying at the Bed and Breakfast called The Bakery in Pulham Market. The host, Martin Croft plays the cello in the Pulham Village Orchestra.

We are starting to gather our own strawberries, three or four a day, and Dad tells me that it is time to begin having our gooseberries (they make a delicious fool!).

Granpins is steadily writing her colonial memoirs which Nina is typing for her. They are so interesting that I will try to get copies for you three. I can remember certain things that she has forgotten such as our armour-plated car in Ipoh during the Emergency — only the driver could see out, and that was through a slit!

20th June 1994

We are most impressed by the Meat Market Craft Centre Gazette. The mentions of you are splendid and most encouraging for you no doubt. The wording of your Melbourne School of Millinery article must have pleased Waltraud immensely — it is so well put together. We are also pleased to see that you are keeping up your interest in puppetry (as we saw from the photographs of your room). We are photocopying the relevant bits from the Gazette to send Christian and Alice who both take an interest in hats and you! Enclosed are smiling photos of them with Nina and Wendy in their wedding hats. Also some Ascot hat pictures from The Times.

We managed to go away for our weekend at a coaching inn on the North Norfolk coast. We went for some inspiring walks on National Trust land. There were lots of fishing boats, rare breeds of water birds, and miles of unspoilt sand dunes. We are looking forward to taking Georgina there some day.

All our roses are in bloom. The first thing Dad did when we arrived back yesterday afternoon was to leap onto his lawnmower!

As Mrs. Pearce had predicted whelks are the speciality of the area we have just visited. Dad had a seafood pancake filled with the most extraordinary things! Back to Beatrix Potter land now with foxgloves in flower under the trees and ducks on the wing.

27th June 1994

We had a very good day on the boat on Thursday — just Dad and me. The weather was perfect so we managed to sail. We took a picnic lunch which the swans were very interested in. The light was good and the silhouette of a solitary grazing horse or cow on the river bank as we looked up at them as we drifted by would have made good pictures. I seem to be repeating the word 'good' but that sums up the day.

In The Times last week there was an article about diet which said that research has proved that Vegetarians are healthier and live longer than other people. I thought you would be pleased!

We haven't watched any Wimbledon this year. It seems to have passed us by. Prudence and Jeffrey are cycling in France this week with friends — in Provence I think. They are going to cycle round a lake so that they can plop into it when they get hot!

10th July 1994

Thank you very much for the exciting first issue of Flashy Hat news. Do we detect your hand in the black and white cover design? Very clever!

On Thursday Arete and Rachael took me out for the day. Rachael drove us through quiet rural byeways to a small family-run business specialising in a wide range of clematis plants. They have recently won a gold medal. There, wandering amongst pinks and purples climbing to the roof of the enormous greenhouse, I chose a deep purple clematis for Dad's belated Birthday present. It has a striking magenta stripe down the centre of each petal which makes it sing. Dad is going to plant it by the swing where it can grow up the old pear tree. Arete also bought a clematis for Dad which he is going to plant to hide some of the mess under the shack by the compost heap. Dad's summer task is to repair the gig house.

There was an article in the Times the other day about buying Scottish castles but it warned that they can often be a trap. When we were driving along in Rachael's car on Thursday we passed a dear little whitewashed former chapel, with a small stained glass window. It is lived in by a solitary bachelor but I thought it might have suited you! We had lunch in Rachael's house which is a former village school with a lot of character and hop-scotch markings in the former playground.

When I used to go and stay with Arete at Warren Hills in the school holidays I used to love the handsome heavy cart horses that were still used for work on the farm then (roundabout 1952).

MacEchern Cinderella coach puppets

13th July 1994

The geraniums on the dining room window sill are racing towards the ceiling! Mrs. Pearce says they are attracted by the light. I have them in pastel as one of my large window scapes for the church exhibition. I have called this series Birds in flight, Lantern on the sill, Sundial with robin and Cool summer days.

Dad wore the wonderful straw boater that you made for him to the Costessey School Sports Day. It won the prize for the best hat and was announced over the loud speaker!

John Halliday is reproducing some old family photos for us. There is a splendid one of your grandfather Noel Nicholls in his kilt with a glorious background of highland scenery for you (next best thing to a castle!).

1st August 1994

I am trying to write this letter in camp at St. Davids. There are quite a lot of distractions, and my page was half-eaten during the night presumably by one of the notorious giant slugs that abound here. We had a good time this morning on the beach at Whitesands. Georgina was squealing with delight at the cold waves and warm

Joan Ells visits Crossingford

sand. We bought her a fishing net for the rock pools, and remembered how William used to play with his Action Man there. Then we each had a hot stuffed jacket potato for lunch at The Old Cross Hotel in St. Davids. Andy bought Georgina a kite which she is already learning to fly. Dad is wearing a French Foreign Legion hat with a back-flap to protect his neck. William and Sara will be joining us for the weekend.

Norman and Mercy's Golden Wedding party was a big success. Before lunch they had a trio on the lawn playing light classical music, and after lunch a jazz band took over. Under the canopy of the weeping cherry tree happy children played. They looked so beautiful and unselfconscious as they climbed the rope ladder and swung from the branches. The village hall where we all had lunch was decorated with massive bunches of white and yellow balloons. I spoke to Rose who asked how you are getting on.

Joan Ells, at whose neighbourly hotel we spent the night at Oxford, said she used to be connected with the upper market hat trade. So she was most interested to see the various leaflets, magazines and press cuttings that you have been sending us.

We have become grandparents again — this time to a tiny new goldfish that has suddenly appeared in the pond! Who its parents are we can't quite make out — or whether it has any siblings lurking under the lily pads? Perhaps the giant orph has eaten all the others?

A bat flew into our bedroom the other night and refused to leave. They are a protected species so you are not allowed to hurt them. Eventually Dad managed to trap it in the curtains and gently shake it out of the window.

June Chantry, a Flowerdew cousin, is writing a collection of hymns. She has asked me to illustrate them.

William and Sara have shown us the video of their wedding taken by a Kodak friend. It is very skilfully done and the sound track is excellent. It ends with a delightful sequence of Malcolm playing with Georgina and a big red balloon. An earlier sequence of Emily dancing with Malcolm is also sweet. Dad and I did not get to dance because Dad was coping with the failing loos, and I was caught up with guests in the dining room and conservatory. So it is lovely for us to be able to relive the occasion on film. You looked elegant.

From St. Davids we all send you love, slugs, seaspray, seagulls and all!

A drinking fountain at Kew in November.

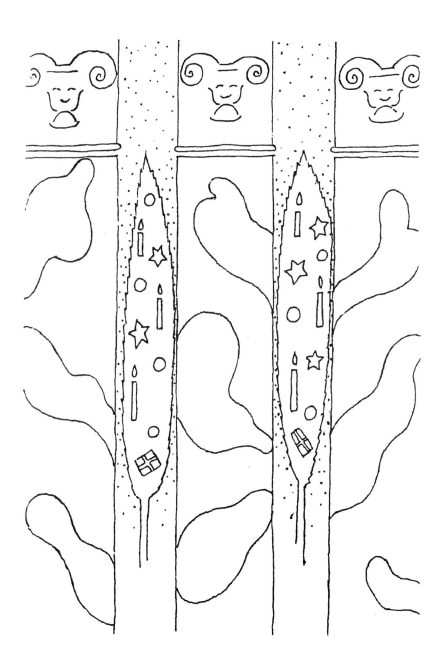

Christmas at The Dorchester 1994

'I dreamt that I dwelt in marble halls' –
With gilded ceilings and silk-clad walls.
The grand piano with nostalgic sounds
To set Joan dancing the second time round.
The lift and wheelchair and corridor long
With carpet glorious and poinsettias strong.
A huge great bed with room for some men
'Five Men Called Moe' might fill it again.
The Christmas trees were many and fine
And to add to the spirit some excellent wine.
Our spacious suite with its pink velvet chairs
And Louis Quinz cabinet welcomed more dears
Such as Prudence and Jeffrey who came here from Kew
To celebrate Christmas with us and with you.
Joan in her evening dress flowing and glowing
Outshone many younger belles toing and froing.
To keep us in order she brandished her stick
But mostly she smiled and kissed us all quick.
The Christmas dinner went on for three hours
Then up to her bedroom to sleep amongst flowers.
The Dorchester grandness had to impress
But mostly Joan's kindness made our happiness.
So its thank you from John and its thank you from Esther
For what was a dream of a Christmas fiesta!

Joan, at the age of 87, hosted a Christmas house party for us at The Dorchester.

The Lantern at the Door

The lighted lantern at the door
Festooned with ropes of frost
Will guide you home at Christmas time
Fear not – you won't get lost.

A welcome warm will wait you there
With loved ones all inside.
The young and old will celebrate
This joyful Christmas tide.

The cats a saucerful of milk
The babe a tiny stocking
The elderly a scarf of silk
And chair a gently rocking.

The stars shine bright this winter night
The lantern softly glows
On ice without and fire within
With coming of the snows.

For those alone who cannot roam
We send a Christmas prayer
That radio or telephone
Will bring more care dear near.

For those who have not got a home
A lantern for to light
We wish a gleaming lamp ahead
God's blessing for tonight.

Snow scene from Crossingford kitchen window

The Life Story of AH Flowerdew

by his elder daughter Wendy Nicholls

My father was a very handsome man with sombre dark eyes. He had a lean athletic figure, and ate sparingly, and did not smoke or drink at all. He and my mother were both extremely fastidious both mentally and physically.

Arthur Harry was born in 1876, and educated at Framlingham College.

After leaving the parental home, Billingford Hall, where his father wanted all ten sons to work on his farms, my father tried various things, and while working as an accountant on a mine in Southern Rhodesia he saved up enough money to pay his way (fees and keep in those days) at the Camborne School of Mines in Cornwall.

At Camborne he was an outstanding man at Mathematics and at all games — soccer and cricket especially. In his Finals he was considered to be one of the best pupils ever trained by the Camborne School of Mines, and he passed second in all England in Mathematics.

In 1913 my parents were married in Lagos, Nigeria, by the Bishop of Lagos. The bride was given away by the Governor of Southern Nigeria, and the Reception was at Government House, Lagos. The Governor of Northern Nigeria was present.

My mother, Nina, was born at 100 Belgrave Road, daughter of Thomas Hoskins, Parliamentary Solicitor to the Great Western Railway. She was an undergraduate at Cambridge University, and, before her marriage, had her own school in Camborne.

After the wedding, the bridal pair travelled north by railway, then by construction railway, then the last day on horse-back, to the mine near Joss of which my father was manager. The 'house' consisted of a cluster of mud huts, thatched, one hut being used as a bedroom, one as a sitting room, another as a kitchen, etc. They were very cool — there is a story of how my mother took the temperature of the kittens' milk with her thermometer, much to the amusement of my father.

Transport was entirely by riding stallions. All went smoothly unless another stallion untethered or unridden appeared. When that happened the form was to slide off one's mount and watch the ensuing fight from behind a tree.

There were practically no white men in the area, and my mother was the only white woman for 800 miles. The only car was stuck in the mud during the whole of her stay. The surrounding Africans were pygmies who used poisoned arrows and were cannibals.

My father then went out to Malaya as Manager of Tronoh Mines, Perak. As he was forty he remained there during the 1914–18 War. In 1918 he went to Kuala Lumpur, where he remained as a Consulting Mining Engineer until 1938.

Then he went to Australia as Managing Director of Tronoh Mines, Harrietville, Victoria, Australia. This mine had the largest dredge in the Southern Hemisphere.

During the Second World War my parents and sister (later Mrs. T.Q. Gaffikin) remained in Australia. My father worked for the Red Cross, and my sister enlisted in the Australian Women's Army where she eventually became a Captain. My mother ran the house with very little help, and with the added burden of myself and my two small children Esther and Dilys — we were evacuees from Singapore when the Japanese overran Malaya in 1942.

When the war ended in 1945, my father returned to England, and from there to Malaya, where he helped in the rehabilitation of the country.

In 1947 His Highness the Sultan of Selangor appointed my father a Justice of the Peace.

After selling the Australian house (85, Ormond Esplanade, Elwood, Melbourne, Victoria) my mother joined my father in Malaya. She strained her heart and died in 1950 in England.

The following year my father married Florence, daughter of Segar Bastard, of Essex. They were married at Oxford, and then went out to Malaya to live in Kuala Lumpur where my father continued as a Consultant Mining Engineer.

In 1953 he retired, and went with Florence to live in a very pleasant house in Nairobi, Kenya, East Africa.

My father loved his daily game (tennis until his eyesight failed, then golf). As the altitude in Malaya was that of sea-level, and Nairobi 6,000 feet, the Doctors warned him that he should play only nine holes of golf. However, he insisted on doing eighteen. This excess, coupled with the fact that he insisted on chopping down a tree one morning when Florence was out shopping, brought on a stroke and he died after a short illness in December, 1953, and was buried in the European Cemetery at Nairobi.

Always known as a man of the highest integrity and justice, he had a wide circle of friends of every nationality. The Mining World brought him into contact with many Chinese, and his interest in Comparative Religion with Indians, and many others.

A versatile sportsman, he played soccer, rugger, golf, tennis and cricket. He was Non-Playing Captain of the Malayan Team which beat the Australian Test Team in Singapore in 1926.

He served the community as a member of the Kuala Lumpur Sanitary Board (afterwards known as the Municipal Council), member of the Committee of the Kuala Lumpur Book Club, as a volunteer up to the age of seventy-six, and helped run polling booths at the first election.

Arthur Harry Flowerdew was a teetotaller and non-smoker all his life. It was a great loss that he died at such an early age as he was writing a book on astrology — this was studied from the scientific angle.

Notes on the Flowerdew family

- The historian Blomfield, who was an ancestor of the Flowerdews tells of the then Billingford squire going forth to bring King Wenceslas' sister to marry one of the Saxon Kings.

- The name Flowerdew was originally spelt Fleuredieu which was a complimentary nickname meaning God's flower.

- A John Flowerdew sparked off Kett's Rebellion.

- In 1584 Edward Flowerdew became Baron of The Exchequer.

- A Flowerdew was Court Astrologer to Queen Elizabeth I.

- A Col. Flowerdew was Keeper of the Tower when the King was imprisoned there during the Civil War.

- A lot of Flowerdews were Puritans, including Temperance Flowerdew who sailed with the Mayflower and married Sir George Yardley, Governor of Virginia, thus becoming the first titled lady in the English New World.

- Sir Bartle Frere has a number of portraits of Elizabethan and slightly later Flowerdews in his home as a Flowerdew married into the Frere family.

- Lieutenant Gordon M. Flowerdew won the Victoria Cross for leading Lord Strathcona's Horse, a Canadian Regiment, in a cavalry charge at Moreuil Wood in France, in March, 1918. He was my Great Uncle.

Nicholls Notes

I never met my Nicholls grandfather, the Rev John Ashplant Nicholls. He was a Minister in the Church of Scotland. I found a newspaper report of one of his sermons which was written at the Cambusnethan Parish Church, based on the text 'Thou didst well that it was in thine heart.' I Kings, viii, 18.

Grandfather's Sermon (extracts)

All great purposes, spite of failure, enrich and ennoble our lives. David, with all his faults, was a better man because of his holy impulse. No man can be utterly base who keeps a place for Divine purposes in his life ... Be not discouraged. There is a glory in failure and a blessing in disappointment.

Solomon, through his father's complete preparations, was enabled to build the temple, worthily and expeditiously — the design was in readiness, the timber, the silver, the gold, the hangings were all assembled, and so the dream of the sire became the achievement of the son. It is ever so.

By our lofty purposes, our self-sacrificing labours, we are making it easier for others to enter into our labours and fulfil for us our unfulfilled ambitions — and we have done well that it was in our hearts to do something for God and for man.

The Rev John Ashplant Nicholls
for his work in hospitals and camps in
France and Belgium 1914–1918
British Red Cross Society

Lorna Tillott
(neé Flowerdew)
Billingford Hall

HAPPY BIRTHDAY

NOVEMBER 5th 1994
WENDY'S 80th BIRTHDAY
CELEBRATION AT CROSSINGFORD
PROGRAM
AND
MENU

Prudence and Jeffrey

William and grand piano

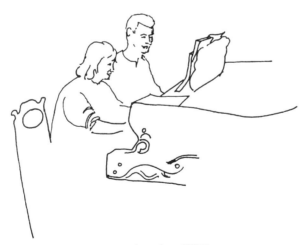

Amanda and William

Wendy's years of accompanying the Pulham St Mary Sunday School

Wendy Nicholls ∾ *pianoforte & theory teacher*

Licenciate, Trinity College, London (LTCL)
Associate, Trinity College, London (ATCL)
Member of the Incorporated Society of Musicians
Member of the International Piano Teachers
Consultants Group
Diploma in Sociology, London University

Crossingford Lodge, Pulham St Mary, Diss, Norfolk IP21 4RJ
Tel: Pulham Market 443

Julianna with Fuzzy on the beach at Coll

Nina recovers

Francis and Nina: at Elly Hill there are beautiful curtains and comfortable swing seats

Bella, 15, at Elly Hill, wearing an outfit she made herself

Rosie aged 13

Golden Wedding Message to Noel and Wendy

Ripening fruit and fallen leaves
Follow after golden sheaves.
For the Autumn time of life
Binds the happy man and wife
In the harvest of their labours,
And the dallying in Love's arbours,
Excess trivia to be shedding
Concentrate on GOLDEN WEDDING.
May it mark a happy time
Full of laughter, music, rhyme.
You deserve some pampering.
It is quite a special thing
To be loyal for so long:
Celebrate it with a song.
Noel and Wendy here's to you
With a picture that E drew
Of fallen leaves and ripening fruit
In glowing colours all to suit
The theme that we are thinking of
Which basically is lots of love.

From John and Esther
Amanda, Catherine and William

Claire's birthday is at snowdrop time

Mathew in 'The Car' 1991

Anthony Rushbrooke

Malcolm: Whizz Kid Boat Cruise 1990

Prudence with sunflower and Mishak at Crossingford

Bold squirrel visits Crossingford

Autumn Song

The Autumn light streams past
The year is waning fast
And bonfires burn at last.
The pumpkin lanterns smile.
Bats hover here awhile
And witches stand their trial.
The stars and moon shine bright
And fireworks light the night.
First frosts grow white and bite.

Remembrance Day draws near.
For those that conquered fear –
A poppy and a tear.
White gulls still stalk the plough
Black crows make such a row,
And trees are barer now.
Hot Summer gone was fine
But colours more sublime
Make Autumn's reign divine.

Before the Winter days
That glimmer through the haze
Rich Autumn we will praise.
To yesterday belong
Its right and also wrong
Its sorrow and its song.
Look forward and look up
With kindness fill the cup –
Give thanks for Harvest sup.

From Esther's Jalan Jalan
to Malaysia 1995

Frangipani trees with their fragrant white yellow-centred flowers adorn the front approach to the hotel, Rasa Sayang, Penang. The back of the five storey building has tropical gardens leading down to the beach. Swimming is not recommended in the sea because of dangerous jelly fish, but the blue pools are attractively landscaped to fit into their garden setting, and a joy to use. Very few people are on the beach at this time of year, but there are interesting sports to watch, such as paragliding above, and horse riding on the sand. A Chinaman in a conical hat performs foot massage on willing guests, and a coconut vendor with a bicycle provides sweet coconut milk for the brave.

> A small boy walks towards me
> Sipping coconut milk through a straw.
> Lovers walk hand in hand
> Along the quiet shore.
> A speedboat noses past
> Throwing up a lot of spray.
> The palm fronds up above
> Shield us from the sun's bright ray.
> An artist paces back and forth
> With paintings up for sale.
> An Indian on a horse
> Rides on the sand – Arthurian male.

When we lived in Malaya, when I was young, my parents took us for a holiday to stay in a bungalow towards the top of Penang Hill. It had to be reached by riding up in the steep funicular railway. We shared the bungalow with my parents' Malayan Police friends Jack and the Hon. Veronica Masefield, and their children Jackie and Delphie. Veronica's mother was also staying with us. I was instructed that I was to be very polite to her and always respectfully call her Lady Hawke. I protested, saying 'Oh but I know her far too well to call her Lady Hawke!' I was ten at the time. Jackie and my sister Nina Dilys were both six. Finola and Delphie were babies. At about this time Jackie and Dilys and I were bridesmaids together in Ipoh. The bridegroom, Peter Rice, could not kneel at his wedding service due to a bullet wound. This was at the time of the Emergency.

The Sultan of Perak and his consort 1948

Malaysia Jalan Jalan 1995

Malaysia Jalan Jalan 1995

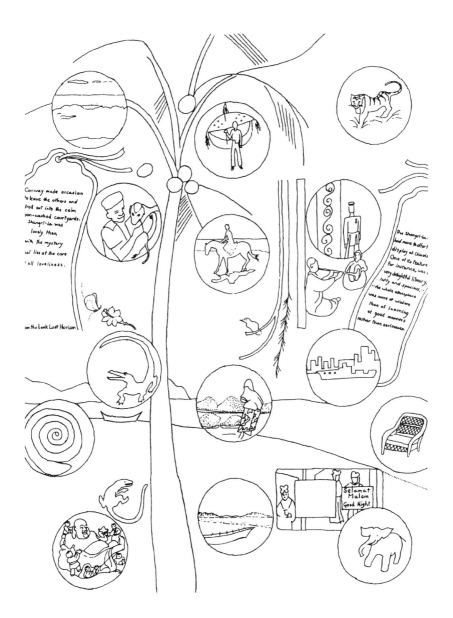

Conway made occasion
to leave the others and
troll out into the calm
moon-washed courtyards.
Shangri-La was
lovely then
with the mystery
that lies at the core
of all loveliness.

om the book Lost Horizon

The Shangri-La
had more to offer!
display of Chinois
One of its feature
for instance, was a
very delightful library,
lofty and spacious.
The whole atmosphere
was more of wisdom
than of learning
of good manners
rather than seriousness

Selamat
Malam
Good Night

John and Esther revisited childhood haunts in Malaysia in 1995

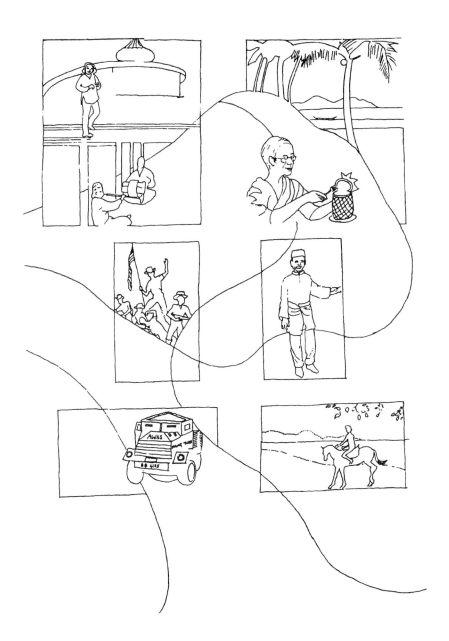

Crossingford Diary — October 1996

We left builders working on the Herschel Room project while we went north to stay with the Simpsons in the Potteries. Mrs Pearce looked after the cats and the tomato plants. The Simpsons took us to see the Birmingham Royal Ballet, and a big garden centre where they bought us a climbing *Gloire de Dijon* rose. They also very kindly took us to the Wedgwood Factory where we spotted a Herschel plaque in the Museum, and the name of Marsden (Joan's father and grandfather) in a written history.

The next day we went to the very grand wedding of Hamish and Louise. On the Sunday we had coffee with Aunt Betty who kept slapping my thigh in a playful way. She was in good form. We had lunch in a pub with Prudence and Jeffrey and Charles and Sara with little Caroline.

We expected to have a rest in which to recover, having got home after 11pm on Sunday night. But first thing on Monday morning the Spanish telescope expert, Rosa, phoned from Bath to ask if she could come and see us that day and spend the night. John duly met her train in Diss to find that she was not on it. She rang later to say she had missed it and caught the next train and would come to us by taxi. She was thrilled with the Herscheliana, and happily filmed Caroline Herschel's dress on the dressmaker's dummy back to front! Rosa flew back to Spain the next day where she is doing research on telescopes for Madrid University.

I then had a tooth out and fainted afterwards, having to be revived by the dental team.

In the meantime lots of dust and noise from the building work. I make many cups of tea.

Amanda rings to say they can't afford to live in their charming cottage any longer so have put it up for sale. Andy is in Finland working on computers.

Cassie rings to say she can't get possession of the flat she wants yet and has been advised to look at other property. She is gloomy.

A brighter voice from William who wants to come and see us but doesn't want to see another paint brush. We ask Mrs Pearce's John if he will decorate the new Herschel Room for us.

The cats are very excited and mystified by the appearance and disappearance of familiar doors, windows and staircases as the building work progresses. They fearfully explore this strange new world.

Old curtains are found in an attic trunk. Why did we keep them? They will surely never do for the showplace Herschel Room. We try to persuade ourselves that they will do. But the donkey grey ones are soon being used as dust sheets.

Last night a colony of Canada geese flew honking and whirring directly over Crossingford — a splendid sight.

Then at 6 o'clock in the morning a crisp silver slither of crescent moon lit the fading night sky.

I have a piano lesson and am given a new book of 'easier' Chopin. John practises the flute then retires into the garden to gather windfall apples and pears. The pheasants have had a good nibble at some of them. Showers of red rosehips abound. A rather comical woodpecker uses his long beak to dig for insects. At night we hear the owl, then all is still.

Crossingford Diary — November 1996

The month of November started with the Pulham Village Orchestra three day Workshop. John, as Chairman of the Orchestra, spent a long time preparing for this. Then in the tutorials he studied to improve his flute and piccolo. Finally there was a concert performance of some of the work studied, including the full orchestra playing two movements of Beethoven's *Symphony no. 7 in A* and *Finlandia* by Sibelius.

Then it was the turn of the Ministry Team to come to lunch at Crossingford where they discussed the usual service of Confirmation to see if it could be improved.

On Sunday John read the Lesson at Matins in our church. It was taken from Proverbs 25 'Like apples of gold set in silver filigree is a word spoken in season'.

We had a visit from Cassie who helped me to make some plum puddings. She later sent us a picture postcard of *November Moon* by Paul Nash, likening it to the colour scheme we are working towards in the Herschel Room.

Seldom seen huge Shire horses are now being kept and broken in on a field near Crossingford. When I was driving up the lane they were being led past and one reared up, dwarfing his trainer, and nearly landed on the bonnet of the car.

We have been experiencing cold, damp, clinging mists, and sharp, white, piercing frosts. But the sunshine when it comes lights up bright jewels on the trees.

Granddaughter Georgina, aged four, is taken regularly to Sunday School by Amanda. Georgina has started ballet classes so I am giving her pink buttons and bows for Christmas.

Grandson Henry, aged one, was christened in June on his father's 40th birthday. Henry's hair is a halo of silky bubbles, and he loves opening and shutting doors.

The muslin gown that belonged to Caroline Herschel is very like those worn in the BBC's production of *Pride and Prejudice*.

My mother loves living with my sister Nina at her herb farm in Darlington. She has her piano, organ and viola there, and a TV and telephone in her bedroom. They have a lovely garden for her to wander around.

John and I enjoyed a holiday in Italy this year, and have just booked to see Spain's castles and orange groves next.

Will's Sara is studying for biology A Level with a view to greater career mobility.

William says that my painting based on Munnings' *Last Cavalry Charge* (led by my great uncle Gordon Flowerdew VC in 1918) looks good on his orange dining room wall.

Our young live near each other and Will and Cassie help Amanda with the children.

The builders have left us to an unaccustomed silence — no more banging, no more dust. We now have a repaired roof, a new safer staircase, a new double-glazed window, a restored tiny door (for Alice?) a new bedroom ceiling with access to the attic, and an improved bathroom. The builders thanked me for their many cups of tea.

A handsome jay comes to inspect the empty nut cage. I must remember to get some more nuts for the birds.

We hope you will have some nuts with your port at Christmas, and a warm welcoming festive season with those you love best. This 'diary' comes, with much love, to offer you a small sample of our year in case we haven't seen you lately, dear.

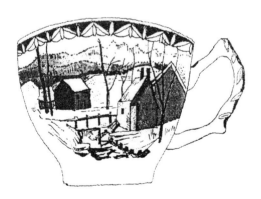

Grandchildren

First Christmas for Henry
What will it mean
A light in the sky
From a star all agleam?

First Christmas for Henry
What will he hear?
The sleigh bells ajingling
As Santa draws near?

First Christmas for Henry
What's that in his cot?
A present from Georgie
Who made the whole lot!

Henry

Crossingford Diary— December 1996

In the first weekend of December John and I went to inspect our youngs' abodes, present and future. There we met Prudence and Jeffrey, good fun as usual, and my cousin Alice whom we hadn't seen for a long time. It was good to catch up on family news.

The Herschel room at Crossingford is finished except for the William Morris curtains.

Cassie flies out to spend Christmas in America with her old school friend, Melissa Henney.

At the Carol Service in our church John reads the lesson 'The Shepherds Go To The Manger'. For once I am warm enough in church wearing my new, long, grey coat.

Our Christmas party for the locals is to be on Twelfth Night. We expect about thirty for hot mulled wine and nibbles. They will be welcomed by a string of coloured lights thrown over the tall Christmas tree planted in our front garden by Finola many years ago.

Amanda and Andy and their two children spent Christmas Day with William and Sara at the latters' smart new house in Farnham.

In January Amanda and Andy are to move to their new little house on a rather pretty small estate nearby. It is surrounded by woods and walks. Georgina has chosen her bedroom which has pink rosebuds on the wall.

William and Sara joined us on Boxing Day. They tried out the new sofa bed in William's (Herschel) room. I had put a vase of forsythia twigs on their window sill (no curtains yet) and two of the small yellow flowers opened for Christmas.

We went for a walk around the garden and paddock with William and Sara to inspect the trees we have planted. The red crab apple tree looks magical. The cats accompanied us on this tour, Gilbert leaping up each tree in turn and performing acrobatics. Sullivan was more sedate.

When we woke up on 27th December there was a white world. We have to keep breaking the ice on the pond for the fish. We notice two empty blackbirds nests in the dormant wisteria. We await the winter aconites which spread a mantle of gold under the big trees in January.

David and Sheila Wilson recently holidayed in Malaysia which they described in their Christmas News Letter to us:

'We agreed to share a taxi. It was driven by a toothless old fellow, Abdul bin Kasim, who told us he was 74 and had a daughter who had studied at London University. Then he said "In year one thousand nine hundred four zero, I joined Singapore Police." So I asked him if he knew Mr Nicholls. "Mr NICHOLLS!!!," he said —taking both hands off the steering wheel and only just missing a passing motor scooter, "Oh, Mr. Nicholls". '

'The long and short of it was that he had known him very well and was delighted to hear about his family again. I gave him a hefty tip and we parted great friends. He was definitely one of "the old school" and thought things had been run much better under the British.'

John and I watched *The Secret Garden* film on TV. It made me cry. We have a fat robin too.

May 1997 be a blossoming year for you — full of good things. And may we see more of family and friends in the coming months.

Designs for Christmas cards

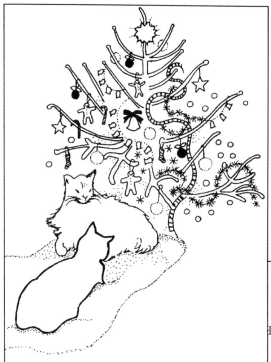

CHRISTMAS

Star Swingers
Carol Singers
Hum Dingers
Life's Beginners
Three Ringers
Snow Lingers
Frozen Fingers
Oven Pingers
Christmas Dinners
Hugs and Clingers
Highland Flingers
Reindeer Springers
Angel Wingers
Dawn Bringers

GREETINGS

Designs for Christmas cards

John Herschel-Shorland plays his flute

Crossingford Diary — January 1997

We celebrated the New Year by having a Twelfth Night Party. A lot of friends from the village came. We gave them hot mulled wine and Mrs. Pearce's cheese straws. David Nix-Seamen said he would like to come and paint the view from our kitchen window. One of our guests couldn't come because her false teeth were being repaired. Otherwise it was a good turnout.

We shopped in the January sales for a new dressing gown and pyjamas for John. We are very pleased with our bargains.

John has been invited to be a Governor of Pulham School. His teaching experience will probably be helpful.

The forsythia twigs that we picked at Christmas are now in full bloom indoors, with a promise of spring.

A letter has arrived from Professor Brian Warner suggesting that we visit him at the University of Cape Town this year. He is an astronomer, and assisting with a production of a book on Sir John Herschel's flower album.

The new William Morris curtains for the Herschel room here are expected at the end of this week. John likes resting up there on the new sofa — so do the cats!

My mother is to celebrate her 60th wedding anniversary on 15th January. She was married in Kuala Lumpur wearing a graceful gown that she had made herself. My father looked dashing in full tropical dress uniform and carrying a sword. They came out from the church through an archway of swords. Christian and Nancy were bridesmaids, and Flowerdew parents and Nicholls mother were there. The sepia photographs are very beautiful.

Amanda is moving house this week. She has taken everything from her larger house and piled it all into her new garage. Her old school friend Penny came and helped by scrubbing out the old kitchen and bathroom. She wanted to scrub out the new ones too, but Amanda had not yet got the key to the new house.

Our piano tuner (who has bought himself an Irish title and appeared as a Baron on TV to prove it) came unexpectedly to tune my grandmothers' grand piano. Once he fell asleep while he was doing it. He has brought it to life, and, with the aid of my piano lessons it is making a much better sound these days.

I watched a Save The Tiger programme on TV about tigers in India being nearly extinct. The next day I bought two cuddly toy tigers, from a charity shop, for the bedroom where our grandchildren will sleep. My nine paintings of tigers hang in the upstairs corridor. Some have been exhibited in Pulham St. Mary Church.

A letter has come from Nelly van der Zwan to say there is a chance that they may be returning to The Grange and if so would I be able to take up our painting together again. I am excited.

There was an article in The Times about Schubert Songs. Sir Thomas Armstrong taught us these when I was at Headington. I saw him on Songs of Praise recently and wrote to him saying what a treasure to take through life his teaching of Schubert Songs had been. He replied in his own hand saying that he remembered me.

The early sunshine in our bedroom lit up the Fra Angelico musician angel card that I had brought back from our holiday in Florence. Later I asked, 'Now where is my angel?' and John's voice replied 'Here I am.'

Today we collected our new car. It is another VW Polo. It is four door, bluebell blue, with a more powerful engine than we are used to so I am a bit nervous about driving it.

We have been swimming again in Diss. The reflections in the pool are reminiscent of David Hockney's paintings. I always follow his career because he is the same age as me.

When I came down to our farmhouse kitchen for breakfast two huge heraldic magpies were at the window. They flew off with an abstract armorial flourish of black and white.

The early morning frosts are silver and white. The remains of the snow lies heaped up on either side of the lane. Our new car has skidded several times on black ice.

The curtains for William's room have been hung. They look very rich. The muslin has arrived from India. This will filter the bright sunlight and protect the pictures etc.

John had his Ministry Team training session at The Rectory last night. One topic discussed was 'What is your idea of God?' Difficult.

The heron has visited the pond several times. The fish are protected by the ice.

We went to a lovely lunch party at Harriet's. There was more news of the van der Zwan's imminent return. Harriet's mother reads Proust in French.

Our Norfolk sun hats have arrived ready for our holiday in Spain. But this is still winter.

Crossingford Pictures

While living at Crossingford Lodge I have done several series of paintings — about thirty teacups, thirty pen portraits of Pulham St. Mary characters, and nine large tigers.

Tiger Poem

Fur fashion – compassion.
Bone trade – dawn raid.
Stalking proud and then a shroud.
Still in fear you prick an ear.
Dried grass – slink past.
Stripy coat and soft white throat.
You leap on prey then gorge away.
Tiger star from afar!
God also made the cool glade.
The creation and intention
Put you here. Don't disappear!
Your beauty thrills in jungle hills.
They'd empty seem without this dream.
Maybe a few survive the zoo.
But nature's child deserves the wild,
The sky and trees and tropic breeze.
Your savage heart expressed in art –
How can we save you? You of brave hue?

Fountain at The Grange, Pulham St Mary

The Fountain

A silver grey
For Christmas Day –
The Child may show
Through frost and snow
A spirit fine
To yours and mine.
A spirit kind
You'll often find,
Especially
Beneath the tree.

Life's fountain's sweet
Where all may meet
The heavenly Child
So meek and mild.
This brings to you
A message true
To wish you well
Where'er you dwell.
For all we pray
On Christmas Day.

Nelly Van der Zwan with drawing pen at The Grange

The clock repairer: from Pulham St Mary portrait series

Orchard at Crossingford

Black Cat in White Snow

The little black cat plays in the snow.
He follows us about wherever we go.

The snow leaves bare branches which wave in the breeze
And menace us darkly like gaunt enemies.

The cars dare not venture to drive up our lane.
The village is washed by a burst water main.

We walk in our gumboots to fetch our supplies
And Gilbert comes with us to our great surprise!

The birds at our window are pretty and sweet
They eat the nuts gladly as their winter treat.

A moorhen lies stiffly so dead in his woe.
We break the ice daily for fish life below.

Like life in a Christmas card? Sadly, oh no!
But life that is different coloured by snow.

Put on the layers of jerseys and jeans
And sit by the fireside telling your dreams.

February 1991

Gilbert on his special mat, one ear cocked

Gilbert by Georgina

Cat Life At Crossingford

Crossingford conservatory:
Crochet, cushions, cats.
Half the time they 'sleep it off'
The other half it's rats!
Rats, rabbits, rodents all
(they never look for bats).
Though rugs are warm and comf'able,
They sleep in trugs and hats.
One is fluffy ginger –
The other smooth and black.
They do not look like brothers –
They often romps and scraps.
But when the evening comes along
They like to sit on laps.

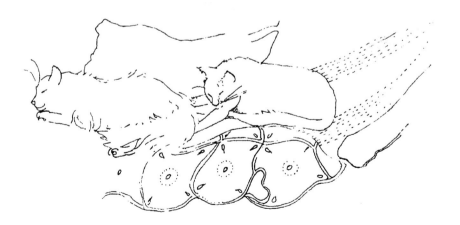

Crossingford Cats continued

Hi! Upside Down High!
Our feet can sometimes touch the sky.
But now on sofa fast asleep
With one eye open we can peep
At cushion creatures upside down
In colours of a cheerful clown.
Arete's patchwork crochet squares
Keep us warm and free from fears:
To snuggle down and deeply purr.
Two balls of black and ginger fur.
We dream of mice and rabbits too
But most of all we dream of you.

Conclusion

Having read through this book and thought 'did we really say or do that?' we are grateful for those times and hope that you, dear reader, whether family or friend, will have enjoyed reading about it all as much as we did in living it. We hope that the illustrations from home-made birthday and Christmas cards will entertain and amuse, the poems too. The plum pudding mix will, we hope, sustain and boost the goodwill that exists among friends and family still. Good night, God bless, sleep well, and may tomorrow bring a more delicious flavour to the pudding of the day.

Index of names

Where relationships are shown, these are to the author. Page numbers in *italics* refer to line illustrations and those in **bold** to photographs.